P9-CEG-070

A
CRACKING
of the
HEART

DAVID HOROWITZ

Since 1947
REGNERY
PUBLISHING, INC.
An Eagle Publishing Company • Washington, DC

Contents

I am exactly who I'm supposed to be

1

You Resurrect the Dead

O n a dark Thursday in March the telephone rang and I
picked up the receiver to hear my youngest child say
"Something terrible has happened," and I knew that a family member was gone.

When death takes someone you love, there is no looking
back. And there is only looking back. You can't complain
there's been a mistake or argue there was no time for goodbyes. You can't protest the life was too short, and you can't
negotiate a deal for a final conversation. When death takes
someone you love, she has slipped off the edge of the world
and there is no bringing her back.

So it was with my daughter Sarah, who was taken from
us without warning in her forty-fourth year, leaving a wake
of vacancy and heartache behind.

More than a day intervened between her collapse and the
time police discovered her body on the floor of her apart-

ment where it lay crumpled by her bed. Though we can never know for sure, it appears she drew her last breath on Wednesday, March 6, 2008. They had gone to look for her after she failed to show up at the school where she taught autistic youngsters, and did not call in sick. It was out of character for her to be unconcerned about her children, so the school called her mother, Elissa, who called my daughter Anne, who said, "We must notify the police."

By the time I answered Anne's call in Los Angeles, they had already located Sarah in the spot where her heart had stopped. For those of us who loved her, there was nothing left but to get on with our grieving and counting up our loss, and then to proceed with the arrangements for putting her lifeless body to its rest.

In the three days that passed before the funeral, I noticed how our conversations kept returning to the final words each of us had exchanged with her when she was alive. What was the purpose of these futile gestures that could not bring her back? Perhaps they could be understood as a desperate hope for the past to flow into the present as before. As though, after the pause, we might pick up the phone to hear her voice, or knock unexpectedly at her door and find her at home to open it when we did.

There were other dimensions to our helplessness during these watery hours—unnerving thoughts that had to do only with ourselves. *I should have spent more time with you when there was time to spend. I should have told you how much I love you, or told you more often. I should have been less contentious when we had our disputes. I should have come up with more ways to protect you. How desperately now, when it is too late, I wish I could put my arms around you and hug you again, and hold you and hold you.*

The reflections of a mourner are a relentless accounting, and there is no bottom line. What words of hers did I fail to understand when she was still there to explain them to me? What did I miss that her eyes were telling me when she fell into her silences? Losing her is too hard, and there is no way to end it.

There are odd synchronicities that appear in our lives when we least expect them. On the last day we can be sure Sarah was still with us, the literary website *NextBook* published an interview with her whose subject was life and death. A note by the interviewer explained, "Sarah died the day after this interview was posted. Our conversation had started with a discussion of how to deal with sudden, shocking loss, spiritually, and I know that the people who knew and loved Sarah are working to do just that right now."

Indeed we were. The "sudden loss" to which the interviewer referred was the death five years earlier of Sarah's aunt, Barbara, whom I had first met when she was only thirteen, and I was courting her sister, three years her senior. In an uncanny prefiguring of Sarah's end, Barbara had collapsed from an aneurism while still relatively young in the New York apartment where she lived alone.

The interviewer's name was Nelly Reifler, and she began by describing her connection to this curious turn of our family fates: "In 2002, my mother's dear friend Barbara Krauthamer died at the age of fifty-eight. Though her death felt sudden and premature, it didn't come as a surprise. For years Barbara had known that she had a congenital disorder, arterio-venous malformation, and that her tangled blood vessels could cause a fatal stroke or hemorrhage at any time. At the funeral, I met Barbara's sister, Elissa and her grown children. All the nieces and nephews were dazed and shocked—but still, each managed to speak about their aunt. Later, at the graveside, Elissa's second oldest, Sarah Horowitz, led the *kaddish*."

Barbara was the relative to whom Sarah felt closest. The two shared creative sensibilities and talents, and a common hand that life had dealt them of struggle against great odds. Barbara was the costume designer for the television series *The Sopranos*, and late in her life had become an accomplished ceramic artist. The intertwining of their fates was a theme of several of the writings Sarah left behind. In the interview she explained: "During my aunt's last years she lived with the knowledge that her life would probably be shortened. She took up pottery, traveled to Italy—just did all the things she'd always wanted to do, so I took that lesson from her. So now when I have an idea, like 'I want to go to Africa,' I don't put it off until 'someday.'"

Barbara and Sarah traveled to Mexico together, and Sarah wrote a poem about their trip:

> *The morning is full of you*
> *the dark ceramic cup you bought*
> *me after a trip to Oaxaca*
> *where we fell in love with*

black pottery
The deep light brown bowl
you made solid and fragile as a
heart
I walk past the cafe where we spoke
for the last time
We had each returned
from places we were warned not to go
We talked about Italy and Israel and
why people no longer fly

When, in accord with Jewish custom, the family unveiled Barbara's headstone a year after her death, Sarah wrote a poem about the event:

Unveiling

One year later
We pack up your things
Stand by your gravestone
Wrapped in layers of clothes
Still bone cold

Reifler noted that Sarah had turned to Judaism in her mid-thirties, and asked whether her religious practice helped her to deal with Barbara's death. "I think it did," she said. "I'm very comfortable with the fact that Judaism doesn't have this highly developed idea of what happens after you die, like Tibetan Buddhism and Christianity. I pursued

Judaism very much to find meaning, and I think at the heart of that pursuit is the fact that we all walk around with the knowledge that we're going to die."

I was finding it hard to take my eyes from the page on which these words were written, and peered at the text as though it were a palimpsest of endless layers. Her thoughts were guiding me towards the future, as though she were my parent rather than I hers: "After my aunt died I discussed it with my rabbi. He was talking about how there are some things that are gone—I'm not going to smell her or have back-and-forth conversations anymore. But he also said, 'Pay attention to the ways in which your relationship continues.' Initially I think that the first part made much more sense to me than the second part. But as time went on, I did come to feel that she's still with me in some way. I can feel her presence sometimes."

The interviewer questioned Sarah about Jewish views of the after-life, which she answered with characteristic candor, acknowledging that "some of the ideas contradict each other." The idea that made the most sense, she felt, was the one called *gilgul hanefesh*, which means a "rolling of the souls," and is the mystical equivalent of a life after life. "It is basically reincarnation" she explained.

Another Judaic vision of the after-life was *olam habah*, which means "the world to come." This one, she observed, was "closest to the Christian idea of heaven, but I think the notion of heaven is a metaphor for communion with God, and hell is basically separation from God. There is also a belief that the souls of the wicked are tormented by demons of their own creation, or are destroyed at death, ceasing to exist. I very much like the idea of the wicked being tormented by demons of their own creation."

There was a third idea, which Sarah didn't believe, that "when the Messiah comes the dead will be resurrected." But she did reveal a fact about herself I hadn't known before: "I say the prayer, 'Blessed are you, God, you resurrect the dead,' every morning over my coffee."

I didn't believe in a messianic resurrection either; but I liked the idea of that prayer over morning coffee. I think now of the resurrection of my daughter in the way her rabbi advised: *Pay attention to the ways in which your relationship continues.*

There was another synchronicity that was not odd, which I discovered in the papers I found in her apartment after she was gone. On a white sheet, creased into four quadrants was this poem:

Heart Murmurs

Some time in grade school we learn that the
    heart
Is not shaped like a valentine. It is the size of a
    fist,
Fills with blood, releases.
We listened to the heart beat the way the first
    drummer must have,
The way cats do when they climb on your chest
    at night.

Irregularities in the heart beat are called
    murmurs.
My aorta is narrow, making the blood and
    breath work harder.
Some have leaky valves and must watch for the
    skipped
beats.
I cannot interpret the screen that monitors my
    heart now.
I can only see the constant rise and fall.

2

God Is Her Inheritance

The call from my daughter Anne came too late for me to catch a plane; there was nothing to do but wait for the morning, when her mother had made an appointment at the Medical Examiner's Office where they had taken her body. Boarding the first morning flight to Oakland, I arrived in the Bay Area at 8 a.m., picked up a rental car at the airport, then made the 45-minute drive up the Bay Shore Freeway to the neighborhood in Berkeley where her mother still lived.

I looked forward to seeing Elissa. Although we had not been married for thirty years, we had not lost each other entirely either. A durable bond had been forged out of the love we shared for our children, and now for their children, and out of memories of a past long gone.

Although the streets of Berkeley were still familiar, they had grown strange enough for me to miss a turn before arriving at her house. I climbed the steps past the rose bushes and bougainvillea in the wintry front yard, their skeletal remains overgrown because the gardener could not bring herself to cut them back. Entering the house I had departed so long ago, I was reminded how different the two of us finally were. In the decades that had wizened us like the vines in her yard, I had occupied fourteen residences in five separate cities. In all that time, she had never left the home we once shared.

Stepping into the interior of wood and leaded glass, I encountered once again its familiar warmth, its elements virtually unchanged. Everything was in its place of thirty years before—the handcrafted furniture still half-hidden in a profusion of plants; the cookware and appliances, among them gifts I recognized from our wedding, the old silverware and china, the volumes in the bookcases, the children's photographs on the wall—all exactly as the day I left. All as when my daughter was still a child.

My heart was already full from the sight of these objects when high on the mantel my eye caught a favorite photograph taken by my mother of the little girl I had once held in my arms. This blast of memory was more than I could handle as a wave of grief swelled inconsolably towards me, then crested, and broke into wracking sobs. When the welter had subsided, I pulled myself together as best as I was able and walked into the kitchen where Elissa was waiting. Together we left the house and drove in the rental car across the Bay Bridge to our appointment, pulling up outside a large complex of gray buildings on Bryant Street which was the San Francisco Hall of Justice.

Inside we were met by the chief medical investigator, a man named Pringle who immediately recognized me from my TV appearances and let me know discreetly that he admired what I did. I was briefly unsettled by this exposure at a moment when I wanted not to be there at all, but thanked him anyway. He handed us a brown manila envelope with Sarah's apartment key, and told us that an autopsy had already been performed. This information produced a second ripple of distress since I knew the procedure was against Jewish custom and worried that Sarah might not have approved. But Pringle explained that the procedure was required in such cases when the deceased was so young and the circumstances unknown. This information afforded a measure of relief since it was an exception the custom allowed. Still, I could not suppress a queasiness at the thought that they had cut my daughter's flesh. When we asked after the autopsy results, Pringle informed us they would not be known for several weeks and might be inconclusive when they were, which proved to be the case.

Our next stop was Sarah's apartment on Anza Street in San Francisco's Richmond District, a neighborhood located near the ocean. Our plan was to collect essential items she had left, including her cell phone and address book, so that we could notify her friends about the funeral arrangements. I was particularly interested in retrieving Sarah's new computer which contained her literary files. This was an iBook Elissa had bought to replace the one I had given her six years before. Sarah was excited by the purchase when I talked to her about it and was already exploring the new capabilities it offered. When we entered the apartment, I caught sight of the old laptop lying on the floor. Sarah had pasted a yellow sticker from the 2004 presidential election across its white lid: "No More Years."

She had lived by herself in this one-room apartment for almost a decade, and there was no task I dreaded more than to enter it now. I was apprehensive not only that the scent of death might have lingered in the place—mercifully, it hadn't—but about the feelings of impotence that always afflicted me when I visited while she was alive. My daughter lived in a small room with a smaller kitchen at the back and a bathroom off to the side. Between the bed in the living room and the table she had set in the kitchen, the area to move about was narrowly confined. The cramped quarters were further constricted by a clutter I can hardly bring myself to describe: papers and books, bedclothes and bags, knick-knacks accumulated over the years and piled one on the other, including the carcasses of three previous computers which were stacked in haphazard fashion amidst the debris. What was a father to do?

But when the door finally opened what I felt was an unexpected relief. Perhaps it was the daylight, which made the room airier and more open than it seemed when I had come to pick her up for dinner only a week before. Perhaps it was the broom someone from the city had left on the bed after cleaning up, giving the impression that no one actually lived there. Perhaps it was the thought that my daughter was now free from this, too.

Whatever the cause my respite was short-lived. It could have been when I was rummaging through her bags in search of the address book, or when I spotted the Alter translation of *The Five Books of Moses* I had given her for her birthday two months before; or possibly it was when I noticed the disjointed pile of laptops on the floor. But suddenly I felt another wave swell and crest, until I had to bolt into the narrow hallway and jam my head against the wall to pull it back in.

While we were locating Sarah's items, my daughter-in-law Felicia arrived. She had volunteered to pick up the address book and cell phone and then make the funeral calls to Sarah's friends, and had driven the forty miles up the peninsula from Los Altos to make the stop and then return. Her sister Jackie had flown up from Los Angeles, and her mother, Loretta, who had lost two of her own children, had also come up to help. The cords of family were being pulled together.

My oldest son Jon had arrived from New York that morning with Renee, the woman who had shared his life for twenty years. On Sunday my wife, April, and my step-son, Jon Kibbie, would be there as well. April had been a powerful support in my life, providing a welcome comfort in my later years, and had made the coming together of our families an effortless blessing. She had opened her heart to Elissa and to my children, especially to Sarah, making her a present of the white painted wrought iron bed she had brought to our marriage. For almost a decade Sarah had written and read and slept in this bed, until the end.

When our tasks were done, we returned to Berkeley and Elissa's house, where we joined other family members and a few close friends. My son Ben had brought along a slide show about Sarah, which he had spliced together from the family photo album. The images on the screen reviewed her life from the time she was an infant until two days before the end, when the last photo recorded her presence at a family gathering at Ben and Felicia's Los Altos home. This final shot, which showed her alive and apparently well, came early in the set, since Ben had chosen not to follow a timeline of her life but to shuffle the moments, moving back and forth from present to past in no particular order. He chose this arrangement because he felt that arranging the images chronologically would have added up to a summary too grim. But the confusion of time in his version did nothing to diminish the effect, which was to bring all the memories of her surging back in one unbearable collage.

For the soundtrack he used a plaintive lyric, selected without an inkling of the meaning of the Hebrew words. A translation was provided by Sarah's friend, Emily, who had flown down from Seattle, where she was a cantorial soloist, to sing at the funeral. Emily recognized the lyric Ben had selected as *L'chalom*, which means "to dream." It was about dreaming one could fly, she explained. "It was so eerily appropriate, being a dream of liberation from a limiting physical reality."

A pretty woman with an Irish sparkle, Emily met Sarah when they were both undergraduates at San Francisco State

University. "We were in a communications class together and one of our assignments was to read a poem," Emily recalls. "No one wanted to do it but Sarah. She read an outrageous poem with expletives by Allen Ginsburg. She had a giant bow on her head and had dyed her hair platinum blonde. I thought she was the coolest person I had ever seen."

As I watched the pictures of my daughter's youth drift across the monitor, a flood of sorrows undid me, and I had to quit the room to hide my embarrassment at being so unmanned in front of my children. When I was able to collect myself, I went back to the viewing, but within moments had to look away again, and realized that for now and long after I would not be able to revisit these memories. Of all the images, the hardest to endure were the ones that had been taken when she was a child, her heart open to a world that had been cruelly set up to put enormous obstacles in her path and eventually to crush her.

For the memorial service Elissa had chosen the Mount Sinai Chapel, which was located on Divisadero Street in San Francisco. In an irony unforeseen, I had attended another funeral in the same Chapel thirty years before. It was the last in a series of political events that had derailed my life, dislodging me from my family, and permanently altering my relations with my children. The service for Sarah was on Monday and several hundred people attended, including her spiritual mentor, Rabbi Alan Lew, who had flown in from Minnesota where he had been visiting family. It began with Emily singing the prayer of mourning,

El Malei Rachamim:
Master of mercy
shelter her beneath your wings eternally,
and bind her soul among the living.
God is her inheritance.
May she rest in peace. And let us say: Amen

I gave the eulogy, pouring out my grief for my lost child, summing up her life as I remembered it. I composed my remarks the day after I arrived in Berkeley, waking myself at three in the morning in the bayside motel where I was staying, and writing it through a hail of tears.

This was my tribute:

Sarah was the sweetest of my children with fine and delicate bones and thick blond tresses that cascaded from under the berets she favored along with the florid bows. As a youngster, she was slender, almost tiny, in a way that made you want to fold her in your arms and protect her. Of my four children, she was also the most reticent. When the four of them were a crowd in the room you would often have to look for Sarah to know she was there.

All parents live to have regrets at the frustrations they vent from time to time, along with the bursts of anger that attend them. And I have mine. But when Sarah was young she was so lacking in willfulness and guile, and her vulnerabilities were so close to the surface that I don't ever remember losing my temper with her. I never knew a kinder person with a bigger heart. While we all begin life with streaks of selfishness and sometimes meanness, such chromosomes seemed missing from her genetic code. Frustrations she had, and anger too, and on occasion she displayed a combative spirit like her father. But I never saw her be unkind to anyone, or to any living creature.

Her lack of complaint was also unusual, and was a disposition that remained with her from the day she was born until the day she was gone. When she was four or five we took the family on an outing to the Oakland Zoo, and made a stop at the ice cream stand. Acting on an impulse that is intelligible to me now only as a reflection of the absurdity of fathers, I decided to make it a life lesson. Perhaps I did so because she was so willing a pupil. "It's important to try new things," I instructed her. "You need to broaden your horizons to see what the world has to offer. Instead of vanilla or chocolate, why don't you try something new like that sour apple flavor, which sounds interesting." I missed the biblical allusion at the time, but I might well have reflected on it. She took my advice without hesitating—she was always such a dutiful child—and chose the sour apple, and we went on our way.

Fifteen minutes into our walk, I noticed that the cone she was carrying had received no more than a lick. So I took it from her and tasted it myself. It was awful. A surge of guilt unsettled me, but we were too far from the stand to go back. In all the time that had elapsed she had uttered no word of reproach, and she never did. I have carried my regret over the incident from that day to this with no hope of repairing it. Of course when I brought it up to her long after she was an adult she just laughed.

When Sarah was in junior high school, she came home one Monday with a long face and tears trickling down her cheeks. When I asked what happened, she was too choked to answer. Then, without a word, she handed me an assignment her teacher had just returned. There were no marks of correction on its pages, but on the cover was a red "F" along with a brief comment instructing her that "plagiarism" was unacceptable. No evidence was provided for this serious charge, nor did I have to read what Sarah had written to know she was incapable of the offense. In all her young years, I had never known her to lie or bend the truth, even about inconsequential childish things.

She had spent the entire Memorial Day Weekend working on that paper. While the family went to a local fairground on one afternoon and took in a movie the next, she stayed home completing her assignment. We pleaded with her to take some time off, but she would not hear of it. She was determined to turn in the best work she could. She was my only child to take her school obligations with that degree of gravity.

After asking her a few questions, I realized what had happened. Her teacher had graded all forty assignments during the Monday class hour, collecting the papers at the beginning and returning them at the end. The time she had allotted was not enough to read them, only to sample their styles. That was why there were no marks on Sarah's paper except for the grade and the single comment. Sarah was a naturally gifted writer, her prose fluent beyond her years, which probably led her teacher to conclude that the writing was too mature for someone so young, or for someone from whom she didn't expect such results.

Taking Sarah by the hand, I went to her school where we found the teacher in her office. Throwing the paper unceremoniously on her desk, I began upbraiding her for making such grave and groundless accusations against a child who had worked so hard to please her. To my surprise, she offered no defense and when my choler was spent, changed Sarah's grade to an "A," making her own behavior even more inexcusable. I never forgot the injustice that had been done to my daughter that day, which made me worry about the hard times that awaited her in the years ahead.

Children constantly press their needs, but in Sarah's case they usually had to be extracted from her. From that day to this. No one in the family knows if her medical problems had worsened in the weeks before the end. Each of us who should have protected her can berate ourselves over this. But we also know there was little we could have done to find out. Defending her independence was the first priority of her vulnerable life, and she fiercely resisted attempts to pry—as she would view it—into her state of health or any other obstacle that might lie in her path.

All her life she faced odds that seemed overwhelming, and not only because she was 4'7"in her stocking feet, which caused many to underestimate her and constantly forced her to exert herself to be taken seriously. From the day she was born she was beset by medical problems that hampered her ambitions. A kinked aorta raised her blood pressure and caused doctors to fear it would shorten her life, and possibly did. She was hard of hearing, eventually almost to the point of deafness in a way that could not be corrected by medical aids. In her first years, she had difficulty forming words because of this impediment, and then putting them together in sentences. Yet she eventually became a stylish writer and, in addition to mastering her own language in a way few are able, made herself learn Hebrew in order to pursue her spiritual path.

She was near-sighted and had a diminished spatial perception along with a poor sense of direction, which made getting places often frustrating and challenging. She was never able to drive, and because of an arthritic hip walked with increasing difficulty and pain as she grew older. Despite these handicaps, to observe the Sabbath in the last decade of her life she walked the two miles to her *shul* and back every week, and sometimes more than once, in fair weather and foul.

Many people would have been discouraged by the difficulties Sarah faced in the ordinary business of her life: the medical procedures she was put through, which often did not work; the frustrations she endured with near-sightedness and hearing aids that fed noise back into her ear, making her pleasures, which were literary and musical, more arduous than they should have been; the impaired mobility which constricted her horizon and made common tasks difficult, from grocery store shopping to taking the bus downtown to service her laptop; the single life which she did not want; the limited finances, which made her count pennies (but never prevented her giving to others), and confined her to studio apartments into which she had to squeeze her things.

But she was never daunted by the unfair hand life dealt her, and never allowed herself to be overwhelmed by its frustrations and disappointments. Instead she made her life an example to those of us who are not so burdened to be aware of our blessings and not be discouraged by our defeats. She packed more interests and travels, more experiences and learning, more friends and projects, more individuals whom she touched in the brief span she was given than most people whose earthly journeys are twice as long. And she left a greater vacancy behind.

A born candidate for dependency, she never allowed herself to become anyone's burden but her own. On entering college, she moved out of the family household, a step that caused anguished concern for her parents, and never looked back. It was not because she was not a family person. Quite the contrary. There was no one more passionate or persistent when it came to keeping her own from yielding to the centripetal forces to which every family is prone. When her heart gave out she was planning a Passover *seder* that would be a family reunion. Instead it is her funeral that brings us together. "What will I do without Sarah?" her mother asked when we mourned over her open casket, knowing there was no answer; "she was my companion and all the goodness in the world."

A few months before the end, I had picked up the phone to call her. It was 8:30 in the evening and I was looking for an answer to a question I had in connection with a project I was working on. My call found her riding a bus home from San Francisco State where she was seeking a Masters degree in teaching special needs children. It was her second Masters, the first having been a Fine Arts diploma she earned from the University of San Francisco a few years before. In the course of our conversation I discovered that it was the third bus she had taken that evening, which meant six for the round-trip to school and back. She followed this routine for three years, working an eight-hour job during the days and going to classes at night.

But it was I—not she—who was unsettled by these travails. On the other end of the line, she was her cheerful self, happy that her father had sought her out for an answer to a question. It was an attitude as integral to her personality as her honey-colored locks and velvet skin were to her physical appearance. Her spiritual buoyancy was also one of her most irresistible traits. She probably never realized what a profound and uplifting impact she had on everyone who knew her.

One of my fondest memories of Sarah is when she stepped up to the *bimah* for her *Bat Mitzvah* service when she was thirteen. She was so short her head was barely visible above the Torah scroll. For the service she had to read the text in the ancient Hebrew, and also sing the "Song of Deborah," who was both a prophet and the first woman judge. Later I came to appreciate how fitting that was, providing her with what was to become her favorite biblical line: "Justice, justice shall you pursue."

Sitting in the congregation, her mother and I waited anxiously for her to begin. Would she stumble over the complexities of the ancient text? Would her cantillation falter because of her impaired hearing? And then her lips parted and there issued into the silence the purest and most true and lovely sound, perfectly articulated and beautifully sung. And it continued like that to the end.

I had a similar recognition when she was an adult and read her work along with several local poets at a neighborhood haunt called the Paradise Lounge. Her mother was in the audience too, as she always was when Sarah performed. Perhaps because she was so small, perhaps because parents are never quite able to let their children go, I felt the same anticipation and concern as she stepped to the microphone. By this point in her life, she had adopted a distinctive style that was well-suited to the stage. On this particular evening, she was decked out in a cocktail dress with a black shawl and black over-the-elbow opera gloves, a black velvet *chapeau* and chandelier earrings—all lit by an impish grin, which she flashed just before she began. There was the same thrill as I listened to her read with a phrasing and inflection that were as alluring as they were professionally pitched, her witty and accomplished texts.

In the last decade of her life, Sarah returned to her faith and became an avid student of the Jewish religion. Whenever I sought her help on a point of scripture or tradition, whether it was to ask about messianic hopes in Judaism or to seek her instruction on rabbinical views of the after-life, I was impressed with the scholar my daughter had become. I could always count on a carefully considered and richly informed response to my inquiries. Many of our discussions revolved around the Jewish concept of a *tikkun olam*, which means a "repair of the world," in which she found a unifying theme for her life.

As she pursued this goal, the causes she came to pursue were the flip side of her kindness, and her compassionate involvement with others. The first family conflict to reflect these concerns took place in her teens, when she confronted her siblings over their enthusiasm for a song called "Short People," which was a savage satire on its subject. (*"Short people got no reason to live/They got little hands and little eyes/And they walk around tellin' great big lies/Short people got no one to love."*) She felt the song was demeaning, but her brothers and sister were naturally amused by her distress over an artifact of the popular culture, and teased her relentlessly. Although heavily outnumbered, she stood her ground and defended her cause, which was something she would be doing for the rest of her life.

The episode proved defining; her battles thereafter were invariably on behalf of "little people" who lacked a voice and needed defenders. As a teen she took up the cause of children who suffered from a genetic disorder called Turner Syndrome, and whom a lazy media regularly referred to as retarded. Sarah herself was a Turner child, which was an indication of how groundless the insinuation was. Later, she devoted her professional life to working with autistic youngsters, and as a journalist wrote a ground-breaking article on hermaphrodites whose gender was defined surgically at birth by doctors who could not consult the infants whose identities they were determining, and who didn't seem to care.

In her crusades she always strove to keep a realistic perspective. She was an opponent of war but recognized that there is evil in the world and nations are sometimes forced to defend themselves. She protested against capital punishment, standing vigil on bitter nights at the gates of San Quentin, but not because she thought the condemned were innocent, as many who came to protest did. She was there because she believed that despite their crimes, which were heinous, it was still wrong for the state to take a human life.

For years, she climbed on a bus every month to go to the Hamilton Family Center on Hayes Street to feed the homeless. It was an obligation her congregation had taken on, and which she volunteered to organize. Every month she cooked a meal for sixty homeless people, taking time to learn how to make meat dishes on the Internet even though she was a vegetarian, because that was what the people she was there to serve wanted.

Despite the enormous difficulties she faced getting anywhere, she traveled to far-away places to offer her help—to El Salvador to build homes for poor Catholics, and halfway across the globe to Uganda to live in a mud floor hut without electricity or running water, to teach the impoverished children of the Abayudaya, a tribe of African Jews. On another mission, she went to India to the slums of Mumbai to seek help for sexually abused Hindu girls. While there she became violently ill, vomiting and dehydrated to the point that her mother, who had accompanied her and was a professional nurse, became fearful for her life and insisted that a doctor visit her bedside. But ordeals like this never dissuaded her from her purpose. To the very end she was planning trips to faraway lands to help others in need.

The Jewish people and their home in Israel were causes she championed, and this was a bond that brought us together. It was not policies or politics that joined us— she always came from the left on these issues, I from the right. Our bond sprang from a common concern for a people whose heritage we shared, who had been persecuted for thousands of years and found themselves threatened again. Sarah visited Israel on several occasions with groups from her synagogue. One of the trips took place in the middle of the Second Intifada, which was spearheaded by terrorist attacks directed at Israeli civilians. To prevent her mother and me from worrying, she kept her destination hidden from us. She told us she was going to take part in a religious retreat on Mount Tamalpais across the Bay, and would not be reachable for ten days. It was only when she returned from the Middle East that she let us know where she had been.

Sarah did not live to see the result of the presidential primary of 2008, but she had made herself part of it. Until this campaign she had been a member of the Green Party, although she was increasingly disenchanted because of its antipathy to the Jews. The presidential bid of Barack Obama, which billed itself as a campaign to bring Americans together, drew her inexorably to its cause. Of course she would be attracted to a leader who didn't fit the normal categories of ethnicity and race, who had written a book called the *Audacity of Hope,* and whose slogan was "Yes We Can." Of course she would respond to someone who reflected in his biography the multicultural backgrounds in her own family, and a campaign which seemed to represent the hopes she had for her country. And of course her father would be skeptical.

But because I knew her idealism was tempered by a sober realism about political movements, when she told me she was going to Iowa to campaign for Obama I was whole-heartedly behind her and told her so. And because she was Sarah there was no way she was going to ask for help to do what needed to be done. So she took her own meager resources and bought herself a plane ticket. She arranged to get herself transported thousands of miles away to a state where she knew no one, to find Jews with whom to pray when the Sabbath came, and to receive marching orders for the campaign. She trudged through airports on her aching, malfunctioning hip; she gritted her teeth and endured the pains of a gastro-intestinal tract ravaged by illness, and she put pressure yet again on a cardio-vascular system damaged and inadequate from birth, and a body waiting to take her cruelly from us only two months later.

Undaunted by discomfort, she marched into a heartland winter, in temperatures of two degrees above zero to knock on doors and bring out Americans she had never met to join in her campaign of "Yes We Can." And you can bet that when she called me from Iowa to report her progress there was a smile in her voice and not a hint of complaint about the punishing cold or anything else.

When the votes were in and a black man had won a presidential primary in a white state, and had gained momentum towards becoming the first African American to be a nominee and perhaps even president of the United States, she relished his success, and along with it, the satisfaction that it was the first political campaign she had ever participated in—and there were many—in which her cause had won.

And in that moment, I was able to share her triumph, to walk across the personal bridge we had built through many years of engagement and contention. "You can be very proud of what you have done Sarah," I said to her when she returned. "Even if they steal the nomination from Obama; even if he wins the nomination and loses the presidency; even if he wins the presidency and fails to deliver on his promises and disappoints you, it doesn't matter. It is already done. America has already been changed forever by this Iowa campaign, and this could not have happened without you and others like you." And what I did not say to her because she would not have wanted me to draw attention to it, would not have wanted to hear it, was that of all the people who came to Iowa to join this campaign, none had done so having to overcome more obstacles or endure more hardship to get there or to carry it through.

A Jewish legend tells of the *lamed vovniks*—thirty-six just men on whom the continued existence of the world is said to depend. (And Sarah would have had something to say about the gender bias in *that*.) According to the legend, God became so discouraged by his creation that He decided to destroy it. An angel came to plead with Him, asking for a reprieve if in the entire world she could find thirty-six just men. In every generation thereafter there have always been thirty-six just men, the *lamed vovniks*, whose presence makes it possible for the world to go on. The *lamed vovniks* are not conscious of who they are, but perform their acts of compassion and justice out of the purity of their hearts. And the rest of us owe the world to them.

You are a *lamed vovnik* Sarah; you are a light in our lives. In the days that were given to you, you set a standard the rest of us can only strive for: To see ourselves in others; to put up lights against the dark; to never relinquish hope.

I miss you terribly, my sweet child, as do we all. Forgive us for not appreciating you as much as we should have when you were here with us. We know this is a fault in each of us. It is the fault in the world, which you struggled so mightily with your small and infirm and embattled being to repair. We fail because we don't appreciate one another enough. To help heal this wound in creation was the meaning you gave to your life.

o   o   o

That was how I ended my eulogy at the memorial service. When I was finished, my oldest son, Jonathan, rose from his seat and went to the podium to speak. He recalled an episode earlier in his sister's life when we thought we had lost her. She was no more than five years old at the time, and we had been visiting the Exploratorium in San Francisco's Palace of Fine Arts, an exhibition hall of science projects. Jon would have been eight, his brother Ben a toddler and Anne a baby in arms, occupying her mother's attention. As usual we had a family dog with us, and one of Jon's friends. After viewing the science exhibits in the cavernous interior, we piled everyone into our Volkswagen bus and drove to Fisherman's Wharf for ice cream. When we arrived and were preparing to exit the car, Jon asked

"Where's Sarah?" and we suddenly realized that we had left her behind.

It was a parent's nightmare. We were flooded with visions of our little girl alone in distress, panicking that some predatory adult might have spirited her away. We hurried back to the Exploratorium and rushed inside, where we found her at the information counter, chatting with an attendant. "It's magic," she said smiling when she saw us, and pointed to the marvels around her.

In his eulogy, Jon observed that Sarah had a different sense of time, and became easily absorbed in her surroundings. This was why she would not have been concerned by the gap when we were gone. He had slightly misremembered a detail of the incident, but made his false memory particularly affecting. In his recollection, we had not driven to the Wharf but had just stepped outside to look at the lake beside the Palace of Fine Arts and feed the ducks. Jon closed his remarks with these words: "If you can hear us, Sarah, wherever you are, and if you can come back, we'll be waiting for you by the ducks."

But this time there would be no coming back. She was lost for good.

A Talmudic wisdom says that when you save a single life it is as though you had saved a whole world. But the opposite is equally true.

3
All the Pain and Love in the World

Coming up on the plane to Oakland I had already begun to think about Sarah's laptop and the book I was planning to put together from its contents. This project had its origins in a conversation a year earlier when I offered to help get her stories published when she was ready. The idea had been on my mind for a long time, but I had not shared it with her until then, because I was not sure how she might react. Years before, I had initiated a similar conversation in an effort that had backfired, so that she had withheld her writing from me ever since. I took her acceptance now as the sign of a new self-confidence, and a seismic shift in our relationship.

The parental bond is a vexed one: the bird must fly from the nest but also land safely. Consequently, a parent's instincts are often at odds with the desire to see his youngster free. In our case, this dilemma was complicated by others also beyond our control. On my side there was guilt towards a child who had so many strikes against her I could not be certain she would survive them; on hers was the stubborn will with which she faced the threats to her independence that never let up. An additional factor was the choice she made to become a writer and thus to compete in a field where I was already established. And there was also the fact that we found ourselves on opposite sides of many political conflicts.

In December 1974, when Sarah was ten years old, a woman named Betty Van Patter disappeared from a local bar in Berkeley, and was never seen alive again. Betty had worked for me as a bookkeeper at *Ramparts*, the radical magazine I edited in the early Seventies. I had recruited her to keep the accounts of a school run by the Black Panther Party, for which I had raised a large sum of money. In that toxic era, the Panthers were celebrated on the left as a "vanguard of the revolution" and were looked on as the innocent victims of a racist state. Five weeks after Betty's disappearance, the police retrieved her body from the icy waters of San Francisco Bay, and I knew in my bones that the Panthers had killed her, as was later confirmed to me by the Panthers themselves. The political community who claimed "social justice" as its cause, and to which I had devoted my adult life, now protected the murderers and posed an immediate danger to my family and myself.

While I attempted to cope with this unsettling reality, other events multiplied its omens. A Berkeley radical named Fay Stender, with whom I was also acquainted, was shot when she refused to smuggle a weapon into prison to help a Panther leader named George Jackson escape. Fay had been an attorney in a celebrated case defending the party's founder, Huey Newton, filing a suit that overturned his conviction on a manslaughter charge. The attack left her paralyzed and terminally depressed over her betrayal and diminished existence. After her assailant was tried and convicted, she took her own life. Shaken again by these events, I attended her funeral service, which was held in the Mount Sinai Memorial Chapel in the same room where I gave the eulogy for my daughter thirty years later.

The series of events that began with Betty's murder led to a crisis of my political beliefs. Until then, the progressive cause had provided my life with its moral compass, but the crimes of those who shared its mission shattered my faith and led to personal chaos and depression that lasted for years. Among the casualties was my marriage to Elissa. I have described the still painful details of this divorce in my autobiography, *Radical Son*, and there is no need to dwell on them here, but its ramifications affected everything that followed—including my relationship with Sarah.

The guilt I felt over the separation from my children prompted me to give them a wide berth—perhaps too wide— in the years after. In particular, I was cautious about inquiring too insistently into personal matters, or encroaching on areas that touched their political beliefs. As a result, my retrieval of Sarah's writings after her death and the post-mortem inquiries I made into her life were a mixture of revelation and reunion that was bittersweet. "When you moved out of house she was sad," my daughter Anne said when I interviewed her for this memoir, "but she didn't have much anger over the divorce. She was much more understanding and grown up about it than Ben and I. We were mad." When I put the question to Ben, he agreed. "She was a lot more mature than we were. She was very determined that we didn't understand the whole story and almost from day one her attitude was: 'Don't jump to all kinds of conclusions. You need to understand everything first.'" I am grateful for this generosity of my lost child, although there is no way I can thank her now.

She was fourteen when I left, and Ben and Anne several years younger, while Jon was already leaving the nest, on his way to college in Los Angeles. I was determined to stay close to the ones still at home, so I moved into a house in Berkeley ten blocks away, keeping up with their school appointments and activities and making them dinner three times a week. Or so I intended. At first, it was difficult to get them to come, and then, when they did, there were constant skirmishes and complaints. Anne and Ben were the ringleaders of the resistance, making jokes about my culinary skills and contriving ingenious practices to shock the occasional guest I invited. But Sarah refused to join this rebellion and was visibly distressed at its stratagems. "Sarah would try to get us to go to those dinners and behave when we got there," Anne remembers. "She would say, 'Dad needs you to be nice to him.' She was always trying to get us to be more respectful than we were."

It was only when she was alone with her sister that Sarah allowed herself to express her hurt and ventilate feelings that were critical. "We made fun of the 'bachelor man,'" Anne recalls, "your sports car, your cooking class, and the movies you took us to every week. One time, you crammed us all into the 260Z and drove us to a movie called *Middle Aged Crazy*. It was about a guy who leaves his family, buys a sports car, and wears cowboy boots. We got a kick out of that."

Six years after the divorce, when Sarah and Ben were out of the house and off to college, Jon invited me to share an apartment with him in Los Angeles, and I eagerly took him up on the offer. Within a few months I had met a woman in the film industry, and married her in haste. Our wedding was staged outdoors on the front lawn of an English Tudor I had purchased in Griffith Park. I invited two hundred guests, including her Hollywood celebrity friends, while Jon's rock and roll band "Candy" played songs he had written on the roof of my garage.

My children had their own views of these adult follies. Sarah and Anne showed up dressed in mourning. "We planned our wedding outfits in black. Sarah was getting into the mean spirit of me. But when we got there she was nice to your new wife, which made me mad. 'We're wearing black to her wedding,' I scolded her. 'We're not supposed to be nice.'" Discussing the event afterwards, Sarah didn't defend the marriage but wouldn't criticize it either. "She just wanted everybody to get along and be happy. I didn't like your new wife, but Sarah's attitude was this was your life and we needed to respect it."

The marriage was a symptom of my chaos and lasted less than a year (as my closest friends had predicted it would), another spiral in the free fall that had become my future. Now that a quarter of a century has passed, I find my children's responses amusing and just. I am touched to tears by my late daughter's concern, but the funereal jest Anne had contrived for the nuptials was lost on me at the time. I was too preoccupied with putting on an extravaganza designed to force a happiness into my life I was afraid might never return.

Even if there had been no such divisive events, Sarah would still have kept aspects of her life hidden from me, as she did from everyone else. When faced with intrusions into the zone of her self-doubt, she was capable of abrupt withdrawals, hiding behind armadillo-like walls for as long as it took to feel safe—if necessary, years. I received a painful lesson in this when I pressed her about a novel she was writing.

At the time she was employed by the YMCA as a preschool aide and was writing band reviews and an occasional article for the local underground press on the side. Her modest earnings from these pursuits did not provide much latitude when it came to choosing a place to live, and Elissa and I fretted over the neighborhoods she found herself in. Even though we were able to offer financial help, it was always limited by an unspoken rule that our gifts should not appear as an indispensable support, which she would have regarded as an assault on her independence.

Consequently, we had few options when she moved into a one-bedroom apartment on Julian Street, a crime-ridden section of the Mission District. One of the poems she wrote described the setting:

These are the People in my Neighborhood

After the Arab shopkeeper who lets us run up
    tabs closes up
After the men who hang out in front of the
    liquor store
are taken away by undercover cops
After the woman in the magic store is through
    telling fortunes,
ten dollars a person
After the woman next door is through hitting her
    kid
and puts her shoe back on her foot
The beat box party goes on

Sarah was joined by two roommates at the Julian Street address. Pooling their meager resources were her friend Andrea and Andrea's friend Mirjam (a Dutch name pronounced "Miriam"). Mirjam slept in the living room, and Andrea took the bedroom. Sarah was left with the walk-in closet, whose space was expanded by a bookshelf divider, which was set a few feet into the room. The arrangement gave Sarah a small walled-off area in the room itself, which did not provide much privacy when Andrea brought home a graffiti artist she had met on the street, who soon became a fourth boarder. "I'm sure it wasn't fun for Sarah to be in a room where this man was too," observes Mirjam. "I remember her voicing her unhappiness with the situation, but it was pretty indirect. She didn't protest; she just made remarks to me."

Mirjam remembers the neighborhood with a mixture of humor and dismay. "We used to call our alley 'the drugstore.' There were dealers on the corner and hookers performing whatever they were doing, and the street always smelled like urine. Around the corner on 16th street there was a bar which was a gathering place for transvestites who drove up in low-riders. The bar had a little stage where the transvestites put on shows and sang, which we occasionally looked in on out of curiosity. One time our apartment was burglarized and Sarah lost a pair of earrings and some deodorant. A magazine my mother had left was missing too, which led us to believe that whoever did it was high on something, because they stole some pretty strange things."

Elissa and I had sleepless nights over our daughter's situation, but there was no way to rescue her from these circumstances. Even the assistance we thought we provided was not always taken, as I discovered long afterwards. Among the items Sarah left behind were stacks of letters, and when I looked through the ones I had written I discovered a note I had sent to the Julian Street address. It read: "Dear Sarah, I know you're hurting a little for cash. I hope this helps. Love, Dad." Inside the torn envelope was the $500 check I had placed there before I sent it. The postmark was dated May 4, 1990. It had never been cashed.

My daughter had made her choices, and I had to make my peace with them. I was careful to suppress my anxiety when we talked, knowing that it would be regarded as parental excess. Her plight caused me to obsess on the course her life was taking, and to worry about what would become of her. She was nearing thirty and barely eking out a living as a teacher's aide. How would she cope if some misfortune should befall her and she was unable to work? What would she do if Elissa and I were not there to provide a safety net?

This was my frame of mind when she sent me a dozen pages of the novel she was writing. The plot focused on a family she had modeled on her friend Andrea's who lived in Fountain Valley in Southern California. Reading the excerpt, I was gratified to see how developed her craft had become. The pleasure of this discovery inspired me to speculate how her talent might provide her with an avenue of relief from the trials she faced. If it were published, her writing might lead to a teaching post or some literary employment, and a job which would include health benefits, which was one of my most anxious concerns.

Consequently, when she called to discuss the pages she had written, I rushed past the praise for what she had accomplished and began asking how long it would take her to finish what she had begun. The pause that followed should have cautioned me that I was entering a fraught terrain. If I had not been so intent on pressing my "solution," I might have realized the danger and stopped right there. But I pushed on instead. I talked about my experience as a writer and how important it was to have "product" if she expected to gain income from her work. Agents and publishers would want to see a volume of output to make the investment of their time and money worthwhile.

Now that so many years have gone by and it is too late to retrieve my words, I realize how far removed from her reality they were. Now they seem as absurd as my advice to a five-year-old to broaden her horizons by choosing the sour apple. Looking back, it is obvious how I had blocked the difficulties she faced just getting to work, and to school, and shopping for her household, and dealing with her health issues. But at the time my concerns seemed urgent and my paternal counsel reasonable and necessary. My blindness was partly a tribute to her success in concealing her difficulties. But it was also because I did not want to confront their severity. The denial was born of the helplessness I felt over her situation, which at times bordered on desperation. Obliviously, I pressed my case. "You write well," I said to her, "but you need to write faster."

Silence followed these words, and then the conversation moved to other things. But without announcing it, she had closed a door. I never saw another page of her novel until the manuscript was retrieved by her mother from the piles that cluttered her apartment after she was gone.

I didn't realize how complete her ban was until years had passed. In our conversations, she would casually mention a poem or story she had written or a public reading she had given, and I would ask to see the piece to which she was referring. There would be a pause, as though she hadn't heard, and I would let the subject drop. On one occasion, however, I persisted and asked her why she wouldn't show me her work. The retort came whistling back: "*Write faster.*"

It was fifteen years later when the unfinished novel resurfaced. She had been accepted into the Master of Fine Arts program at the University of San Francisco and, as one of the requirements for the degree, she had to finish the work I had never seen and submit it as a thesis. At first she called her fiction *The Family of Man*, but later changed the title to *The Carousel of Progress*. Her idea was a typically insightful one that while we seemed to be advancing, generation upon generation, we were really going round and round. It was a classical idea with a conservative drift, and I liked it.

Her narrative was set in the 1970s, and was about a dysfunctional family from culturally radical Berkeley, whose father, like Andrea's, had lost his mind. While the family patriarch is hustled off to a mental institution, the mother and children re-settle in conservative Garden Grove, a city neighboring Fountain Valley in Orange Country. Sarah had changed the location to protect Andrea's identity. The story was told largely through the eyes of the three displaced and fatherless children and was a perfect expression of Sarah's fascination with life's endless mosaics. Garden Grove was also her friend Emily's home town, and Emily drove Sarah around its neighborhoods as part of the research for her book.

Sometime during the year that Sarah was enrolled in the Masters program, I came up to San Francisco to hear her class read portions of their work. Sarah chose a passage from the novel. Once again I was impressed with her talent and the maturity in her writing. Once again I pleaded with her to relent and let me read what she had written, and once again she said no. At the time, I noted to myself that she took equal pleasure in my desire to see what she had written and in telling me I could not. I had my own ambivalent satisfactions. Each time she denied me access to her work I felt a pang of rejection. But it was accompanied by paternal pride in her self-assertion. I felt another kind of satisfaction when Elissa and I attended her graduation in December 2002 in a pouring rain, flowers in hand, and I caught her smile when she saw me coming.

In the years that followed our phone call, Sarah eventually had second thoughts about the ban, enough to show me a few stories. When she sent them to me, I was pleased to see that she invariably signed her work "Sarah Rose Horowitz," inserting the middle name we had given her to remember my grandmother. One of the stories was called "Two, Three, Many Vietnams" and was about capital punishment. Another was a love story with a Vietnam theme that she titled, "Remove Shoes Before Entering," a reference to the practice at Buddhist meditation centers.

Years earlier, she had made an exception to the reading ban when she sent me a poem that had appeared in *The Berkeley Poetry Review.* It was presented alongside offerings by such well-known poets as Thom Gunn and was the only poem she wrote that was ever published. The poem was called "Ambivalence," and in it she described her father as "an angry ex-Marxist and neo-Republican," and then said, "As a result I can hold my own with both communists and right-wingers." The poem ended with a reference to a *Time Magazine* cover story about her generation: "We were described as whiny and ambivalent." I was grateful each time she lifted the ban and let me see something she had written. But she never did show me the novel, even after she received her Masters degree. When I asked about it, she said a bit peevishly that it wasn't finished, and she was going to work on it when she had time.

This history formed the backdrop to her acceptance of the offer I made in the year before she died to help her get her stories published and the pleasure I experienced when she did. In the many months that passed after our exchange, I never questioned her about how she was progressing with the manuscript. I had learned better. But just before she left for her Iowa campaign in December, she called to ask me about the length a publisher would require of a manuscript before considering it for publication. Her question told me the project was alive and I answered that there was no set length. I had published a short memoir called *The End of Time*, which contained a little over 30,000 words. She said she thought she already had about two-thirds of that in hand. Very well, I said. Let me know when you're ready, and I'll be there to help.

This was why on the plane to her funeral I was thinking about the contents of her laptop and how I would make good on my promise. I was anxious to give my daughter in death the gift I could not give her in life, but I also wanted to be practical. I was aware of the difficulties I would face in interesting a publisher in the shorter writings of an unknown author. These difficulties would be even greater for one who was deceased. On the plane ride between Burbank and Oakland, I considered the idea of putting together a volume of all her writings in a private publication for family and friends, and calling it *The Book of Sarah*.

I began to have second thoughts about this course as soon as I set to work on the eulogy for her funeral, which like all writing was an act of discovery for the author himself. In the papers we had retrieved from the apartment and in her emails to me, which I revisited while working on my text, I began to see my daughter in a new light. When I delivered the eulogy and then published it on the Internet, I saw how a brief portrait of her remarkable life could be an inspiration for others. People from whom I would never have expected such reactions wrote to tell me how they wept on reading her story, and how uplifted they were by her example—by her personal courage and her passion for others.

I received the following note from my friend Sherman Alexie, a Spokane Indian and a gifted American writer:

Oh, David,

I send my prayers out to you. And songs. I just came back to your email from a funeral. My best friend lost his five-year-old daughter to a heart condition. And, in mourning, my best friend took out his hand drum and sang a song for his daughter. It was a gorgeous wailing tribal song. I think I was hearing all the pain and love in the world. And in reading your eulogy for your daughter, I heard that same gorgeous wailing tribal song; once again, I heard all the love and pain in the world. Your daughter was an amazing person, David, and your last words honored her.

Responses like this made me reconsider my plan to put together a private collection. There would be time enough for that. I saw now that her writing was only one dimension of what she had to offer. There was a spiritual lesson in her life, in what she was able to achieve against great odds, and also in the narrative of our efforts, father and daughter, to understand and reach one another. This was a story that deserved an audience, and I resolved to tell it.

4

Her Own Set of Lyrics

Sarah was born in London on January 4, 1964, in a one-bedroom basement flat near Hampstead Heath where our family had taken up a residence that was to last several years. According to the English practice, a midwife delivered her at home, and a doctor came to look in on her the following day. During the examination he noted that she had an extra flap of skin on her neck and her hips were dislocated. He prescribed splints to remedy the hip problem and later returned to inform us that the flap on her neck was an indication of a rare genetic defect known as Turner Syndrome, which was caused by missing cells in one of her two x chromosomes. Among the life consequences of this condition, according to one medical encyclopedia, are a wide and webbed neck, low-set and curled ears, low hairline, small stature, swollen hands and feet, drooping eyelids, dry eyes, cataracts, obesity, diabetes, infertility, arthritis, middle ear infections and, less frequently, hearing loss (which in Sarah's case was progressive and severe), heart defects, and high blood pressure. Early death. The encyclopedia notes that there are no known preventions or cures.

Characteristically, Sarah refused to have her webbed neck and drooping eyelids and curled ears corrected by plastic surgeons. She endured more than one elaborate operation to restore her hearing, which failed. When she reached adolescence, she was given hormones to create female characteristics such as breasts and menses but which, as a side effect, piled on unwanted weight. Because the hormones did not make it possible for her to bear children, she considered adopting one as an adult. On reflection, however, she rejected the idea—not because she didn't want a child, but because she was afraid she would be unable to provide for one.

As a result of her constant need for medical consultations, she soon acquired a distaste for hospitals and doctors, and a skepticism about their ability to provide remedies. For years I tried to persuade her to get a hip replacement for her arthritis, especially after having had a successful one myself. When I saw her limping and recalled the pain of my own degenerating joint, I pressed my suggestion, but failed. She was waiting for a less intrusive option, which she had learned was on the way.

Despite her frustrating experiences with the medical profession, she was conscientious about her doctor visits and understood that the coarctation of her aorta, which raised her blood pressure to dangerous levels, was a threat she could not ignore. She was dutiful about getting her checkups, and since her mother and sister were both nurses I was confident that she was being as well looked after as possible, despite her natural resistance to being looked after at all. Eventually, medicine again proved itself an imperfect science, this time with consequences that could not be reversed. Among the papers she left behind was a hospital report from her last check-up, which she had received a month before she died. It indicated that she was doing well.

Among the life-long afflictions she suffered were ear infections caused by her deformed Eustachian tubes, which made her virtually deaf. She was prone to stomach flus which were common ailments in the dank San Francisco winters. To these were added the occupational hazards of colds and sore throats picked up from her children in the pre-schools where she worked. Her recurring ill-health was a source of constant frustration to her, but she was able to summon a good humor about it. When I asked what she was taking for a particularly aggravating cold, she replied, "My favorite: 'Wal-tussin.'" This was a Walgreen knock-off of the cold medicine "Robitussin," but because I had never heard of it, I thought she had made the name up. The reference became a standing joke between us, which helped to avoid the irritation that could intrude on any conversation about her health.

The way she dealt with her hearing was a reflection of the inner fortitude that sustained her throughout her life. It was manifest even in her recreations, which could be contentious. "Sarah was always super competitive in our games," Ben observed in the eulogy he gave at the funeral service. "She was the same in conversations and arguments, always aggressive, never held back by any insecurity about her abilities." One of the children's favorite games when they were young was a musical contest devised by Jon, who would one day become a musician himself. He would play songs on the family stereo and ask the other three to guess the titles. Since Sarah was hard of hearing and Anne was too small to compete, Ben enjoyed a decisive advantage. Consequently, he was surprised when Sarah occasionally won. How she did this remained a mystery to him, until one day he told her she didn't have to sit so close to the speakers as to be virtually inside them. "It's the vibrations," she explained.

When the two of them were alone, Anne and Sarah developed their own version of the record game. Anne would write down a line from a song, and Sarah had to guess the rest of the lyric. "Because she was so hard of hearing, Sarah often got the words wrong," Anne remembers. "She had a whole different set of lyrics to the songs, which is the way she thought things were."

One of the artists Sarah was drawn to was the English singer Elvis Costello, then a counter-cultural icon. "For us, Elvis Costello was the embodiment of the sensitive guy, only without being a wuss," observes Emily. "He was tough and funny and smart. Being tough and funny and smart made him a hero to us because it is an attitude that allows one to cope with suffering and to create beauty from sorrow."

Anne and Sarah collected his albums and went to see him perform live at Berkeley's Greek Theater. One of Sarah's favorite Costello lyrics was a song called "Red Shoes": *"Oh I used to be disgusted/and now I try to be amused./But since their wings have got rusted,/you know, the angels wanna wear my red shoes."* She was also fond of the song "Radio," an attack on the commercial medium that singers like Costello depended on to reach their audiences, but whose normal product was bland and the antithesis of his own: *"I want to bite the hand that feeds me/I want to bite that hand so badly/I want to make them wish they'd never seen me."* Such sentiments resonated with the rebel streak that had already become integral to Sarah's outlook.

She was eighteen when she went off to college at San Francisco State, where she took up residence in the dorms. There she met friends whom she would keep for the rest of her life. Among them was Emily, whom she met in her first year. "I wanted to have a good time," Emily says of her attitude then; "I wanted to hear bands." Sarah was eager to join her, and the trips they made together to the local clubs became her favorite social engagement. They went to shows in North Beach and the Haight and "tried to be hip and cool." One of their favorite haunts was the Mabuhay Gardens—the "Fab Mab" they called it—which was a band venue with a bar. Several of their friends came along. "They were cooler than we were," recalls Emily. "They had perfect outfits, while we remained hangers on and never really got it together. Part of the reason was that neither of us could be bothered to focus that amount of time on our hair and dress."

Another college friend who became part of their set was Elizabeth Janes, who remembers Sarah in the cultural idiom of their generation as "neither retro nor punk, but unto herself." Elizabeth felt that Sarah's tiny size helped her to stand out, but what really made an impression was how she presented herself. "I remember her in a pastel pink outfit from head to toe, and I remember thinking that for someone so small and with her shape to wear that outfit and carry it off was something else." Attempting to get their bodies trim, Elizabeth and Sarah took an aerobics class but felt like "fish out of water." Elizabeth thought yoga suited Sarah better, "although she had to be careful because her body was inflexible in certain parts."

Elizabeth was a writing major, interested in poetry. Sarah had already determined on a literary career but didn't enroll in any composition courses herself. The two women eagerly compared notes, and talked about their mutual interest. In Elizabeth's view, writing was Sarah's "preferred mode of communication" because "it took her away from her physical limitations. It was a true representation of her mind without being clouded by anybody's superficial reactions to her appearance."

In her second year Sarah began keeping a journal, an indication of the seriousness with which she approached her ambition. She would continue this practice to the end of her life. On one occasion, when they were discussing her writing, Emily said to her, "It's really cool your dad's a writer too. Maybe he'll help you." The comment produced an immediate reaction: "No way. I'm going to be a writer on my own, and I'm not going to be getting help from anyone."

Emily and Sarah left school before graduating, leaving their unfinished requirements to be completed later. Together they moved into a tiny studio on Haight and Fillmore. It was the first of many apartments that Sarah would share with Emily and other roommates. All of the apartments they lived in were located in the Mission and Fillmore districts along the 22 Bus line, which was an indispensable component of their choices since none of them drove. Finding an apartment on the 22 Bus line became the first priority in any apartment search. After that, the necessities were proximity to a grocery store and a pharmacy, and if possible, some local night life. The buses had to run late enough so the women could return home after the evening was over. The 22 Bus met all these needs.

Every time they moved, which was often, they would throw their belongings in garbage bags and get on the bus. "When we finally were able to rent a two-bedroom flat on Valencia in the Mission," Emily recalls, "we were so excited to have such a big apartment, we just started schlepping immediately. You should have seen the drivers and all the people on the bus giving us stink-eye as we hauled all that stuff up the bus steps, and held everybody up."

Buses were crucial to other aspects of Sarah's life. She needed them to get to her jobs, which were dispersed throughout the city, and to get to school where she was taking credits towards a Masters in special needs education. Yet when Emily proposed to her that she apply for the reduced fare passes, which were available to people with disabilities like hers, she wouldn't hear of it. Emily never did succeed in convincing Sarah. It took some brusque arguments by her sister Anne to wear her down. "I said to her, 'You're disabled, and you don't have money; you need to get a bus pass.' She snapped back at me 'I'm not disabled.' I said, 'Shut up you're disabled and I'm getting you a bus pass.' It took nearly five years for me to persuade her to sign the application, but she finally did."

All of Emily's arguments with Sarah were over such issues. "Sarah was really easy to live with, the best roommate I ever had. We listened to the same records, didn't care about the messes we made and were very happy together. But she'd get mad at me when I hassled her about her health, or when I said, 'You are utterly qualified to get Social Security payments for people with disabilities.' That would really steam her. 'No,' she would say. 'I'm not, and I'm not going to do that.'" And she didn't. Anne kept up the pressure but in the end failed to persuade her. Anne still possesses the original Social Security application she requested for Sarah, which Sarah never signed.

"Sarah pretended there was nothing wrong with her all the time," Emily recalls. "Once I said to her, 'You get a lot of ear infections.' And that was how I found out she had Turner Syndrome. Her disabilities were visible, yet she was in denial about them. She wanted to carry on as though they didn't exist. She didn't want to make any adjustments because of them, and she didn't want anyone talking about them."

Sarah, about 3 years old

Sarah, about 6 years old, Jon, and Ben

Sarah, about 10, and Anne

From left to right: Sarah, Erica, Elizabeth, Emily, Andrea, and Roger at Elizabeth's wedding at Black Point Battery Park, San Francisco, October 18, 1991

Mirjam, John Jackson, and Sarah, circa 1994, when Sarah was 30

Andrea, Emily, Donald Brenner, Mirjam, Sarah, and Elizabeth in the Haight apartment, circa 1989

Master of Fine Arts,
December 2002

Rabbi Lew, 2007

Sarah at a religious retreat. Rabbi Lew is in the background, circa 2007

Elissa and Sarah at the last family gathering, March 3, 2008

Sarah at a Purim celebration, March 2007

Photo courtesy Brian E. Geller

Emily Katcher   Sarah, 2008

Sarah and Mariah

Sarah, Mariah, and Julia

Sarah in El Salvador
with American Jewish
World Service, 2003

Sarah in Uganda with the Abayudayah children, 2004

Sarah at Obama campaign headquarters in Iowa, December 2007

Remarkably, her determination to be independent didn't seem to affect her sympathies for others who lacked her grit. In a characteristic gesture she wrote a sympathetic poem about Nancy Spungeon whose boyfriend, the punk rocker Sid Vicious, stabbed her to death during a drug-infused argument. The director Jonathan Demme made a film about their iconic career and sordid end, called "Sid and Nancy," which was released about the time Sarah and Emily moved into the one-room apartment on Haight. In Demme's film, Spungeon is portrayed as an insufferable nag who provoked her own destruction. Sarah's poem sprang to her defense.

Nancy

Some people are doomed from the womb.
I was born with my umbilical cord wrapped around my
Neck, like the rope my mother tried to hang herself
With when Sid killed me.
I always knew I'd die young and in headlines.
They made a movie about me. I was portrayed as whiny
and manipulating.
They forgot that I'd read many books and, at times,
Was kind to those who cared for me.
They forgot that I was loved, that my mother repeatedly

Dreamed of me at five, with tracks on my arms,
  crying
"help me, help me."

Sarah's neighborhood in the Fillmore was a rough urban terrain, bustling with drug traffic and addicts, though not quite as menacing as Julian Street. "We loved the place on Haight and Fillmore," Emily says, brushing aside the negatives. "You could walk right outside and there was a natural foods store, a Walgreens, a great coffee shop, a bookstore, a Thai restaurant, and hipster bars, where we went to hang out." The bars had names like Noc Noc and Mad Dog and featured local ska and rock bands and imported beer. During the days the two women taught nursery school for minimal wages and at night Sarah took classes and worked on her teaching credentials at San Francisco State. On the weekends they visited the clubs, or, if Emily had a date, Sarah would stay home and read. She took time to jot down notes in day books, recording her observations of the people she encountered, and analyzing the characters and situations in the stories she was working on. The words she put on paper created a world she could control. Through endless hours she wrote and re-wrote her texts, and her career as an author developed at a deliberate if slow pace.

While living in the Haight, Emily and Sarah re-united with their classmate Elizabeth who was working at a bookstore in the Mission called Small Press Traffic. Sarah visited the store frequently, and the two began trading their favorite underground authors and titles. "Sarah was more adventurous literarily than I was," says Elizabeth. "She introduced me to the poet Nikki Giovanni, the only 'mainstream' author I would even read." Inspired by the reunion, Emily and Sarah laid plans to move to a larger apartment and expand their household. They recruited a fourth roommate in Andrea, who had been Emily's friend since childhood.

The four women soon located the two-bedroom apartment on Valencia Street. To celebrate its spaciousness they christened it the "Maxi Pad." They laid out their futons on the hardwood floors, and converted the existing living and dining rooms into separate bedrooms. They had no other furniture to speak of, but found a typewriter table on the street and used it as a dining table. "It was tiny," Elizabeth remembers, "but it was an upgrade from the cardboard box Emily and Sarah had used before." On the rare occasions they entertained, they rolled up the futons and converted the room into a reception area. Other than the holidays, they didn't do any cooking that might be called elaborate. "We were all vegetarians and ate pinto beans every single day," Elizabeth recalls. "When we ate at home we were eating cans of beans and when we ate out it was burritos with beans."

Like other young people, they spent a lot of time talking about the future and what they were going to do with their lives. But the focus of these sessions wasn't the usual speculation about husbands and jobs that might await them. "We weren't sitting around thinking about mates or careers," says Emily. "We didn't talk about that. We talked about what we believed in, what we wanted to be a part of, and what we felt was right."

Eager to understand the world they were entering as independent women, they were voracious consumers of newspapers and television shows, notwithstanding their ambivalence towards the latter. "We viewed television as a bad addiction," Elizabeth recalls, "but at the same time we were also hungry for knowledge of people different from ourselves." Sarah owned the only television in the apartment, but she let Elizabeth, who was the only smoker, keep the set in her room so she could enjoy a cigarette when she watched it.

Some of the discussions they engaged in touched religious themes. "We were all spiritual seekers," says Emily, whose family were Unitarians. "That's one of the reasons we were all friends. None of us had settled convictions; we were all full of questions. We spent a lot of time looking at the spiritual side of things." Among the questions they entertained were, "Is there a God? If so, what is God? What role in this world does He play, if any?"

When Elizabeth moved on from the Valencia household, Mirjam joined as the fourth roommate and became a participant in the discussions, which continued when they moved to the Julian Street address. "All of us were searching at the time; I was going through a lot of darkness then, and so were Sarah and Andrea," recalls Mirjam. "We were wrestling with questions of self-worth and self-esteem, and going through periodic depressions."

Mirjam was an attractive woman, but was dating a man she had met on the street. "He was half-Apache and half Salvadoran. He was a drunk. I found out later he was dealing cocaine in Dolores Park. What was I doing with a guy like that?" she wondered later. As difficulties developed in the relationship, Sarah stepped in as Mirjam's confidant and support. When Mirjam discovered she was pregnant, her boyfriend agreed to accompany her to the clinic where she had scheduled an abortion. But at the last minute, he informed her he wouldn't be going. "Sarah came with me instead and was there when I had the procedure. Before we left, my boyfriend showed up carrying ropes. He said he was planning to abduct me and the baby and take us to the reservation. But he was too late; it was already over. So Sarah and I just left. I have no idea why I was involved with someone like that. The fact that I was, showed that I was in a really bad place."

Sarah's problems were different but also troubling. She was depressed about her body, and the loneliness it seemed to impose on her. When her roommates were out with men, she stayed behind and read or wrote in her notebooks. Mirjam's good looks allowed her to have dates regularly, often as many as four times a week. Sometimes she could feel that Sarah resented her social life and the men she went out with. "It never came out in hostility. It was just in the tone of her voice, and a feeling of hurt I got from her. On the other hand, she didn't let her disappointments discourage her. She was extremely determined and stubborn about where she wanted to go. She always knew she wanted to be a writer, and that kept her moving forward."

The neighborhoods along the 22 Bus line provided stimuli for her literary ambitions. The Albion Club near the Valencia apartment showcased local musicians. Around the corner was the Dover Club, a celebrated haunt frequented by artists and writers, among whom was my former *Ramparts* editor, Warren Hinckle, who wore a pirate eye-patch and always came with his dog. Over beers, the women chatted about their lives and shared cracks about the locals who turned up. Every so often, Sarah would drop out of the conversation to take notes and store up material for her fictions. "Sarah was constantly collecting characters," recalls Emily. "We'd sit around a table and talk about our lives, and the people in the cafe and the dumb boys we dated. And then those people would show up in her stories. She had an ear for conversation, even though it was hard for her to hear what people were saying. She was never without a notebook. She would pick up a particular turn of phrase and open her notebook and just write it down. The more the years went by the more she wrote. It became a thing for us to buy her 'blank books' with fabric covers and elaborate designs that had just become fashionable. We would buy her one whose cover reflected the colors she wore. We would say, 'Oh, that one's Sarah pink' or 'Sarah purple.'"

The main agenda of the evenings out, they all agreed, was to have fun. On one occasion this consisted of ordering three Long Island Ice Teas instead of their usual beers. Elizabeth thought of this as a "splurge event," since the beers they usually nursed were so much cheaper. They sipped each other's "teas" to see if they tasted different, which they did. "With one drink we got so plastered that we sat there for three hours because we were so scared to move, even though we lived across the street."

One of the attractions at Small Press Traffic where Elizabeth worked was an open mike night in the evenings at which local poets read their work. Similar events were put on by other clubs they frequented. With Elizabeth's encouragement, Sarah ventured onto the poetry reading scene. "I encouraged her to do her first reading at the Paradise Lounge, but she really wanted to be out there and didn't really require much pushing. Emily and Andrea and I came along to clap." After leaving Small Press, Elizabeth acquired a new job serving coffee at the Intersection for the Arts, which was also a site for readings. Yet a fourth venue was "Brainwash," a combined laundromat and café south of Market. The idea was "do your laundry, hear a band, and listen to a poetry reading. Sarah really got into the readings. When she performed, she usually wore a beret and scarf, something really soft; velvets and silks; crushed velvet; purples and deep reds and things like that. It was a high spot for our entertainment calendar when she was on." At the readings, her roommates would squirm uneasily in their seats. "She would read stuff, and it would be so embarrassing to us," Emily remembers, "because it was about real events. We'd all poke each other and say it's about *you*."

The young women cast themselves as a commune of bohemian artists. Elizabeth and Sarah were writers, and Emily was the lead singer in a band called *Barefoot Contessa*, whose musical style was billed as "post-punk folk-rock." *Barefoot Contessa* played at The Blue Lamp, the Hotel Utah, and The Albion, and at the locations where Sarah and Elizabeth read their poems, like Paradise and Brainwash. For their on-stage costumes they wore their ordinary street clothes, which were anything but ordinary. "We all tended to look like a thrift store exploded," says Emily—"lots of black, sometimes jeans, and sometimes not." The black set off Emily's Irish complexion, a dramatic tie-in for her dark brown hair.

The public readings proved to be Sarah's element. She read with gusto and panache, relishing her moment in the spotlight. The poems celebrated her environments, and reflected her interest in the people she observed in the cafes, on the street, and in her life. Among them was this description of the Mission neighborhood:

Open Fire Hydrants and Urban Children

*Heat settles on her skin. She imagines peeling it
    until
she is only heat. She craves the food of hot
    countries;
tacos with extra guacamole, falafel with real
    tahini sauce.*

*She thinks of open fire hydrants and urban
   children.*
*There are some smells, like the smell of wet
   cement*
*That she cannot separate from childhood.
   Summer will*
*Always taste like peach ice cream and sound like
   ally ally all come free.*
*She is no longer ten and even childhood has
   changed.*
*It's full of things she doesn't understand, like
   Nintendo*
and Ninja Turtles.
*She watches the neighborhood children now
   sucking paletas*
And smiling through their brown, sticky faces.
*The moment is long, like the days are now, like
   dreams*
That linger long after you've woken.

Another described a scene from the Fillmore:

Straight Out of the Fillmore

*"Button up your coat. It's cold here in the
   Fillmore,"*
A mother snaps at her son.
Caged trees struggle against the wind,
Faces shut like windows,

And up the street a man screams
"You owe me money motherfucker!"

But the readings that really roused her audiences were in this vein:

Warning

Make-up should come with warning labels:
This product invites men to approach you on the
    street,
grab your arm, comment on your tits, make wet
    sounding
kissing noises, invites men to follow you saying
    hey
baby, don't be like that.
You lean closer, breathing your beer soaked
    breath in
my face. I hold my own breath and count the
    seconds
until the bus comes, minutes until the bus comes.

Many of Sarah's writings described the experiences of the people she lived with. Mirjam, who had a cancer surgery, was particularly taken with a story in which one of the characters went through a similar ordeal. "The words the character used were not words I had ever said," she recalled later, "but were extracted from what I had said, and made sense to me. She took my thoughts and put them into a line about how life sometimes hurts more than surgery."

Sarah never wrote directly about herself. This reticence was closely observed by Elizabeth, whose attitude was disapproving. It eventually became the point of a contentious discussion which took place long after the Valencia household had been dissolved. The two were standing on a street corner in the Mission when Elizabeth brought up Sarah's readings and the fact that she never addressed her audiences in the first person. "I told her she ought to put herself into her poems. She needed to describe the insight she got from her uniqueness. She never addressed that in her writing. I thought her audience would eventually reject her if she didn't examine the political impact of her size and appearance on the view she had of the world. There was a lot of confessional poetry on the circuit at the time. It was quite the fashion. So I thought I had this going for my point of view. But Sarah rejected it as a form outright. She said she would never write that way. She felt that if she focused on herself in her poetry, she would turn herself into a sideshow act, which was something she had been fighting her whole life."

The conflict was heated, and their relationship never really recovered. Elizabeth regretted the estrangement and never quite understood it. She remained fond of Sarah and came to the funeral to pay her a final farewell. When the service was over, she helped Elissa and Anne remove Sarah's things from the apartment. "While Annie and I were cleaning up after the funeral I thought about that argument," she says. "I realized I had never made allowances for Sarah's physical limitations. I should never have engaged her in that discussion when we were standing out in the street. She probably didn't hear half of what I was saying."

The hardest defeats Sarah suffered in her struggles to avoid becoming a sideshow were the ones she endured in her efforts to have a normal social life. The fact that there were other women occupying the same apartment created opportunities to meet new friends but also to experience new disappointments. "Sarah was always game to go out," recalls Emily. "Wanna do this? 'Yah.' Anybody else would be like 'I wanna check my calendar.'"

Elizabeth was something of a loner. "Sarah and Emily had a lot of friends together," she recalls. "I didn't bring new people to the group. I was a witness to their social life. And Sarah was a witness to Emily's social life." Elizabeth thought Sarah's high standards contributed to the problem. "Whereas Emily was open to relationships with all different comers, Sarah was extremely selective. She didn't want just anybody because she didn't want them to date her merely because they were needy. She wanted them to fall in love with her."

In a story fragment she wrote while living on Julian Street, Sarah examined the lives of two women with Turner syndrome whom she called Jennifer and June. In Sarah's text, June confides to her friend: "It's hard for me to get out of bed each day—really hard—and nothing happens once I get up that makes it worth it. When do you stop being mad? When do you stop feeling cheated? When do you stop saying, 'Why *me*?'"

The two women attend a conference on sexuality where a speaker tells them they "have to make peace with [their] bodies." Raising her hand "wildly" Jennifer asks: "How do you do that? I try very hard but then I read studies describing us as 'abnormal-looking,' and people make stupid comments, and no matter how cute I dress I can see the way men's eyes glaze over when they see me, and I want to scream."

Returning home, June finds a videotape in her mailbox. The tape is the record of a wedding she had recently attended. She puts the tape in a player to view it, then sits down to write an entry in her diary: "I was incredibly embarrassed to see myself on video. I see how short I really am, how fat my face is, how little the chin I have, and the beginnings of scoliosis in my shoulders. I also made the really attractive gesture of rubbing my nose with my lacey white glove. It's really hard for me to deal with what I really look like. I hate my body. It's that simple. It embarrassed me. I feel deformed. I feel stilted. And I don't feel that way inside. Inside I feel thin and gregarious, sexy, serious, and composed. How do you make peace with your body? *I want to know*."

In family conversations the subject of boyfriends could prove touchy. "She got really mad at me when I asked her if she had one," recalls Anne. "Then she said, 'If you must know, I do.' The person she named was a tall blond kid we went to school with. At the thought of the disparity and what I saw as the impossibility of the relationship, I started laughing and that really ticked her off."

In her talks with Emily, Sarah sometimes confided her loneliness and desire to meet someone. When she went on a date and it didn't work out, she took it hard. "She'd be heartbroken, so upset. I fretted about her. The attitude she eventually adopted was that she was unlucky in love. She referred to herself as 'the in-between-chicks'-chick.' But she also consoled herself with the idea that there was something universal in her experience, that men and women were ill-starred matches. She saw a lot of us go through the same routine. Men would want us, and then they would leave us. We would talk about love and the failures of love. Then we'd start making fun of ourselves."

To vent their frustrations, the two of them papered an entire wall of the Haight Street apartment with posters featuring punk bands that had gothic names like *The Children of Pain* or *Flowers of Pain*, or *The Suffering*. "The band lyrics were melodramatic and self-dramatizing—'my life is misery' and stuff like that," laughs Emily. "We thought that was really funny. So we made a wall of it. We called it 'The Wall of Pain.' We asked everybody to bring flyers. We hung up dead roses. We thought it was hilarious. Sarah and I both had a black sense of humor, which not everybody got."

When Sarah was living in the Maxi Pad on Valencia Street, Andrea's brother Joel came up to see his sister at the beginning of a Thanksgiving Weekend. He had planned to go back to Fountain Valley for a family dinner the next day, but his car broke down, and he ended up spending the week in the Valencia apartment. Joel was a stockbroker and an amateur songwriter and guitarist. Sarah showed him around the city and fell in love with him.

"It was a pretty magical week," Joel remembers. "We had an affinity in the way we looked at the world and a common sense of humor that was slightly perverse. We liked to greet each other with the salutation 'Hail Satan' to make fun of the blue noses who took such things seriously. Who could take *that* seriously? We made fun of liberal hypocrisies and conservative ones. The snarky, sarcastic, tongue-in-cheek jokes never stopped. We had the same twisted sense of absurdity. I was attracted to her because of the amazing fabulous girl she was, compassionate, funny, wickedly hilarious. We rode the bus together all over San Francisco.

"She *was* San Francisco for me. Everything I ever did in that city was related to her. We had no money so we went to libraries and the *Imaginarium* and thrift stores and used furniture stores. At night we went dancing. I even ate her vegetarian stuff, but only because she made it. We discussed her writing. She told me that in many of the stories she wrote she was using my family as material. Presumably because my family was the most screwed up one she'd ever run into."

He found her determination and sense of adventure infectious and a spur to his own ambitions. He played his songs for her, and she convinced him to play them at the Albion that week. At first he was hesitant. He had never exposed his songs to an audience of strangers, and he was anxious about how they might be received. But Sarah persisted, and he yielded to her prodding. The performance was a better success than he expected. "When it was over, Sarah said to me 'I told you so.' That was a big gift she gave me. Afterwards, I started a side career as a musician and have been playing clubs ever since."

When the week was over, Joel went back to Los Angeles. There would be other times they were together—when he came back on occasional short stops to San Francisco, or when she visited April and me in Los Angeles. But it never went further than that. Separated by hundreds of miles, their encounters were limited to occasional chats on the phone. Whenever these occurred, Mirjam noted how animated Sarah became on her end of the line. But the friendship never went beyond that.

"She wanted more of a relationship, but I said no," Joel observes ruefully. "It's the greatest shame of my life. I wasn't man enough. It was my greatest single failing as a human being. I fell in love with Sarah that weekend, and I wasn't man enough to overcome my male desire for a hot-looking twenty-year-old. I loved Sarah deeply. I don't know why I was so weak. I loved her to death, and then I came back to southern California from that week and I was hundreds of miles away. I met someone and married her. A few years later, the marriage ended in divorce. As I look at it now, my relationship with Sarah was the most natural, close, most rewarding friendship I ever had. But when I met her, I wasn't in my forties and smart; I was in my twenties and stupid. I let happiness get away from me. I should have married her. I think about that all the time. The times I spent with her were so intense it was like yesterday. I can see her now with that huge smile reaching up to give me a body hug. And then that giggle and 'Hail Satan.' She was so smart, so good. I will miss her forever."

Sarah's women friends were less forgiving and felt that Joel was insufficiently mindful of her particular vulnerabilities. "She spent years hoping the situation would change," Emily says, "just wishing that it would work out. Then he told her he was getting married, and that broke her heart."

Her sister Anne felt that most of her love poems were really about Joel.

Desire is Fruition

Walking after sunset
sidewalk supple
and solid
beneath my feet
Your voice like dusk
Words sure as
touch touch fluid
as words
the brush of chill
air against my
cheek

No Words

I have no words I told you in my dream
You caressed the nape of my neck
like fire heat on a rain soaked night

Awake

I wrestled limbs caught in limbs
like words in a throat
I saw a zafu burning
The zafu burned but was not consumed

Awake

we stood outside enveloped in night
I miss you I said
It was Shabbos and it was raining
You had no words but eyes full
as rainclouds
In a dream
you woke me
with a kiss
tender as a
wound

In love as in other matters, Sarah told pieces of her own story in her fictions about others. One of the short pieces she left is about a young woman named "Shauna," which is based on a real occurrence that happened to Andrea but has obvious overtones related to herself. The story opens: "Shauna lay on her bed, arguing with God. 'Why did you give me the desire, and the capacity for love, if I have to be alone?'" Shauna makes a "pact" with God: "If I can't have what I want, I don't want anything to do with men."

But this resolve doesn't last, and she soon finds herself falling in love with an Iranian student who works at the fast food place where she is employed. After the two get to know each other, the young man informs her that his visa is expiring, and he'll soon be deported. He is worried that if he is sent back home he might be drafted into the Iranian military. Shauna offers to marry him so that he can get a green card and remain in the country.

"You would do that for me?"

"I should tell you first that I have feelings for you beyond friendship."

"I have the same feelings for you, but I can't get involved right now. If the situation in Iran changes, I want to go back, and help. It wouldn't be fair to involve you in that."

Shauna tells him that she would be willing to marry him anyway. After the wedding they move in together and live under the same roof for awhile. Shauna quits her job and enrolls in a class in Farsi, the language of Iran. But when her husband receives his green card, his true feelings emerge and he asks her to move out. Stunned by the rejection, Shauna agrees to do so, but then returns to confront him.

"You said you had the same feelings," she said, moving her hair behind her ears.

"You misunderstood me. I didn't mean it like that."

She felt her breath escape in long, silent, exhales. I've been deluding myself, she thought.

In an effort to recover from her failed marriage, Shauna flies to San Francisco and moves into an apartment on Valencia Street shared by two of her friends. As the story moves towards its conclusion, one of Shauna's new room-mates invites her to take a walk around the neighborhood. They pass a bus stop where three homeless men are sitting on a bench, drinking wine and accosting passersby for spare change. Her roommate suggests they take the bus to the beach. As they proceed towards their destination, "Shauna felt that part of her was still sitting on the bus bench with the homeless."

The story ends: "The beach was cold, not like the warm, southern California beaches. Shauna watched the waves of the Pacific moving back and forth, over and over. She could feel gravity returning to her body, like the slap of the wave on shore."

Sarah's writing about love wasn't all mournful. When I was finally able to read her novel, I came on a passage about two lovers that contained a hymn to the marriage she never had. It was part of a letter that one of the girls in her fictional family wrote to her missing father telling him about her love for a young man named Patrick. The letter opens with a memory taken directly from the life Sarah and I shared:

Dear Dad,

I think of you whenever we play Mozart. I remember that you loved Mozart. I remember driving to school, listening to the classical station and trying to guess who the composer was. I practice the flute several hours a day now. I love the repetition of it, going over and over the same notes. But it's not the same song at all. Each day it changes, the notes are clearer, smoother. The texture changes too. Like the dawn it changes from day to day. I love waking in the dark stillness, then watching the dawn come in, all chaos and creation. I've been going to mass with Patrick. I haven't told mom. I can hear her listing the sins of the Catholic Church like a catechism: Galileo, crusades, indulgences. Have you noticed how prayer makes the day more vibrant? It's hard trying not to control everything, but I'm learning to let go. It's better though, isn't it, to let your life unfold like the dawn? Each weekend Patrick and I feed homeless people at the church shelter. I feel almost guilty about the pleasure it gives me to chop vegetables, knowing they'll go to someone who's starving. . . .

I fell in love with Patrick at the mall. I tried on pairs and pairs of jeans and none of them, none of them, fit. Every time I turned around in that airless dressing room, I was face to face with my naked body and it was like I was thirteen again, desperately hating my own flesh. And I started to cry. In public. At the stupid mall. So I collected myself, collected my things, but Patrick saw that my eyes were still wet. "Forget about it," he said. "You were made in the image of God, not fashion designers."

Last night he took me to a Chinese restaurant and wrapped inside my cloth napkin was a gold ring with tiny blue sapphires. I imagine marriage will be something like mass. There will be the daily-ness, the sameness of things, and yet the shape of marriage, like the shape of mass, will change everything.

Reading this passage, I am struck by the way the spiritual path Sarah embarked on in the last fifteen years of her life infused her vision of all things. Her comparison of the routines of marriage to the repetitions of the mass could equally apply to the rituals of the Jewish calendar which evidently governed her days. In this phase of her journey she had also come to a peace made possible through her faith, which provided her with a mission larger than herself.

She had continued her friendship with Mirjam, and the two still met occasionally for tea and catch-up sessions. By that time Mirjam had married and become a high school biology teacher. "What I noticed after Sarah started going to the synagogue," Mirjam recalls, "was that a lot of the anger I had seen beneath the surface before was gone. She was finding a lot of beauty in life. She was as stubborn and determined as when I lived with her, only now it went into her spiritual practice, and her spiritual practice seemed to have a profound impact on her life. Not living in a closet with a guy on the other side of a bookcase in bed with her friend might have helped. I would ask her about her love life, 'Is there something going on?' And there was now often someone she was interested in, not necessarily romantically, but as a friend. There seemed to be more connections for her."

5

Some Things
There Are No Words For

In 1995 when Sarah was thirty-one, she moved into an apartment by herself on Bush Street. It was the first time she had set up house alone, and also the first time she was going to live in a neighborhood that was relatively safe. She was working as a teacher's aide for special needs children through the Golden Gate Regional Center and as a researcher at Pacific News Service, a progressive media organization. She was also writing occasional pieces for *The San Francisco Weekly*. In February 1995, the *Weekly* published a cover story under her by-line, titled "The Middle Sex."

Sarah's feature was about hermaphrodites and began with a quote from the Roman poet Ovid: "The nymph and the boy were no longer two, but a single form, possessed of a dual nature, which could not be called male or female, but seemed to be at once both and neither." What followed was a report on people whom nature had made different, and who were put into familiar categories by others who were regarded as "normal." This was a very personal issue for Sarah, and not the first time she had confronted it.

When she was seventeen her doctors at the University of San Francisco Medical Center provided her with the phone numbers of other women in the area with Turner Syndrome. Sarah contacted them, formed new friendships, and found a cause. Accompanied by her mother, she attended annual meetings of the national Turner Syndrome Society and joined its local chapter, the Bay Area Turner Syndrome Society or BATSS, an acronym in which she took special delight. She began interviewing Turner adults with the idea of writing a book, and left behind many tapes from the unfinished project. Her intention was to make the lives of Turner females familiar to others and to do what she could to counter discrimination against them. Her article on hermaphrodites expanded the mission as she took up the cause of another genetic minority at society's margin.

She began by interviewing a woman named Cheryl Chase who was born with an enlarged clitoris that resembled a penis. For three days doctors debated Cheryl's gender and then decided that she was a boy. But a year later the same doctors determined that Cheryl had the normal xx chromosome of females and was, in fact, a girl. To make her a normal looking girl, they ordered a surgical procedure to remove her clitoris-penis. After the operation, Cheryl no longer had sensation in her clitoris, and experienced no orgasms as an adult. "The first thing people ask when you have a baby," Cheryl told Sarah, "is 'Is it a boy or a girl?' and the answer's not allowed to be 'I don't know' or 'in-between.'" Cheryl's observation provided the template for Sarah's article, which was an inquiry into whether society should make room for "in-between" genders. She surveyed the attitudes of all concerned—parents, doctors, and "inter-sex" people themselves.

Re-reading Sarah's article years later, I am impressed by the journalistic integrity of her work, the fairness with which she treats all the actors, including the doctors who performed the operations. It was so characteristic of her attitude. A decade after her article appeared, an intersex activist from San Francisco named Hida Viloria was a guest on *The Oprah Winfrey Show*. The show aired just before Sarah left for Iowa and her last campaign. Viloria told Oprah that while she knew she was different, she had not known there was a word for what she was or that there was a community of people like her until she read Sarah's article in the *San Francisco Weekly*. Sarah's article inspired Viloria to become an activist, championing the right of intersex children not to have their gender surgically pre-determined, and not to have a male or female gender assigned to them, despite the medical profession's advice that leaving them to remain as they were "would unnecessarily traumatize the child."

Citing a psychologist who warned that "we don't live out-side a culture," and shouldn't expect doctors to be cultural revolutionaries, Sarah responded with a reminder that the responsibility of a doctor is first to do no harm. "Clearly when doctors say that it can be painful and even devastating to grow up intersexed, they're right. But plenty of other conditions can cause physical discomfort or psychological distress, and some evidence suggests that intersexual identity doesn't have to be traumatic." She then cited a study which reported that a significant number of children who were raised "intersexed" had been found to be well-adjusted.

But the most poignant evidence she marshaled was the testimony by members of the Intersex Society themselves who told her that "meeting other intersexuals has been a profound step in accepting their own identities." At the end of the article, she introduced her readers to an intersexual named Dave. "Despite Dave's extraordinarily painful childhood, he has come not only to accept his intersexuality, but to see it as fundamentally liberating. 'Since you're neither gender, there's a kind of freedom in that,' he says. 'You can make your own rules.'"

Sarah saw her own self with a clarity that grounded her views of others and made her a fierce defender of those who were born different. Occasionally she would express to her mother a wish that she could be normal, but she never shied away from standing up for who she was. Her determination to embrace differences and to assert a oneness of the human family was an overarching theme, guiding her work for the Bay Area Turner Syndrome Society and drawing her to similar causes throughout her life.

Three years before the article on intersexuals appeared, Sarah had become interested in yet another birth anomaly when Ben's second child, Mariah, was diagnosed as autistic. The diagnosis was made when Mariah was two years old, and the news at first depressed Ben until a friend reminded him that "it wasn't my daughter who had changed, I had." Sarah liked this comment. She was in a position to appreciate better than others, as Ben observed, that "while the autistic label might change one's perception of a person, it was still the same person."

The effects of autism vary from child to child, but in Mariah's case the condition was fairly severe. She would not look at others when they entered the room and remained unaware of their presence while they were there. As soon as her condition was diagnosed, Ben embarked on a search to find his daughter the best therapy available. He soon settled on the behavioral techniques developed by Dr. Ivar Lovaas at the UCLA Medical Center. Lovaas was of the opinion that intensive therapy had to be provided in the first three years, while the brain was still developing, for the prognosis to be good.

Unfortunately, this required professional attention eight hours a day, which would have been prohibitively expensive for Ben, then a struggling executive with a growing family and a modest income. Since Ben could not afford to pay a full-time Lovaas trainer, it occurred to me that I could hire Sarah, who was already working with special needs children. I was single at the time and able to spare enough funds to replace her salary as a pre-school aide and cover her frugal living needs, which Elissa was also (and always) available to supplement.

The idea afforded me additional pleasure because I knew this was a way of supporting Sarah that she could accept. But I also knew the initiative had to come from Ben. So I called him with the proposal, he called Sarah with the offer, and the deal was set. She would get on a bus in the Mission early in the morning and take it to the Cal Trans station in San Francisco, then ride the train down the peninsula for nearly an hour until she reached the stop in Mountain View, where Felicia would pick her up. Then she would work a full day with Mariah and get on the train again.

Sarah was methodical about the tasks she set for herself. She went through the Lovaas training but also did her own research about autism and the methods for dealing with it. She acquired a skill in sign language, and studied different therapy techniques, selecting the ideas she found useful. "As determined as she was, she was also pragmatic and open-minded, Ben recalls. "The Lovaas people were aggressive about wanting us to mainstream autistic kids like Mariah. Sarah was not so sure. She had been around the deaf community a lot and was familiar with their attitudes on this subject. There was a movement in the community that deaf people should be taught by other deaf people, which Sarah found attractive." After weighing the practicalities, Sarah came to the conclusion that forcing autistic children to be mainstreamed was probably not the best idea. Ben agreed, and Mariah was placed in a special needs class.

Either through instinct or through her training Sarah had acquired a heightened understanding of behaviors generally. When she came down to Los Angeles to visit April and me,

she had to confront our two Chihuahuas who were boister-
ously anti-social. The little dogs would bark ferociously at
visitors and sometimes nip at them when they felt their ter-
ritory had been invaded. This was particularly true of the
one we had named "Lucy." On one occasion when Sarah
approached, Lucy erupted in a canine rage. In a lightning
response, Sarah seized both her legs, flipped her on her back
and began stroking her stomach while issuing soothing com-
mands. The stunned animal fell immediately into a trance-
like state, and from then on was a model of hospitality
whenever Sarah came.

Sarah put her experiences with Mariah into one of her
fictions. The story was called "Joseph" and was about an
autistic baker whom the narrator, who is one of his co-
workers, describes simply as "an unusual guy." The story
provides a glimpse into the way Sarah understood people
who could not make themselves heard by others.

Because of some kind of neurological disability, [Joseph]
couldn't communicate verbally. Years of special training
taught him how to read and follow a recipe. Because he
needed visual cues the recipes were printed up for him in
large type and tacked on the walls. There were instruc-
tions specific to him too, like 'No licking,' 'No putting
warm rolls on your cheek.' Joseph wasn't truly mute. He
babbled to himself constantly; sometimes you could
make out actual words. When he was very excited, like
when a fresh loaf of bread was coming out of the oven
he squealed and flapped his arms. Joseph communicated

by typing into a computer. His messages were short and to the point: 'Need flour.' So Joseph's silence was not a true silence...

When Joseph was little his mother took him to the top specialists and they all said the same thing. There was no remedy for his condition, and she would have to institutionalize him. They advised her to focus on her other children. But the mother resisted: 'Can you imagine? Such a beautiful child and so damaged. But I knew that he was a bright boy and he could learn.' At first she didn't understand him. 'He would get so frustrated when he couldn't say what he wanted, like he would want a bagel but I wouldn't know that, so he'd bang his head against the wall. Oh that used to frighten me. But then we put pictures of his favorite foods on the refrigerator and he learned quickly that if he gave us a picture of a bagel he would get exactly that. That was the end of the head banging.'

The details of Joseph's behavior were drawn from her real experiences with Mariah, but along the way her narrative took a leap to become a parable of what she thought unusual people like Joseph could teach us about ourselves. In her story, two of Joseph's co-workers at the bakery—"the kind of guys who wore too much gel in their hair and had tight T-shirts"—took to teasing him. "'Hey Joseph, you got a girlfriend?'" one of them named Jeff taunted. At the time, Joseph was taking loaves out of the oven. "[It] was his favorite part, and he was doing this thing that sounded like scatting. He kept doing that as if Jeff hadn't said anything. But then he stopped and went over to the computer. 'I don't understand women,' he wrote. 'Women always change their minds. Bread never does. I prefer bread.'"

The narrator recognizes Joseph's silence as a refuge he has sometimes created in his own life and in particular in a conflict with his girlfriend Courtney:

> When I first met her at this pizza place we both worked at, I found her chatter soothing, like a warm quilt. And our silences were light, like risen bread.... A year later our silences were different, loaded with things I didn't want to say, even to myself. Once, towards the end of our relationship she was in bed with a terrible migraine. She asked me to go for some Chinese take-out. 'Ok,' I said. 'What should I get?' 'Oh, anything,' she said, waving her hand lethargically. I went to the Chinese place on the corner and looked at the yellow menu in the window. The words swam together, and I couldn't seem to make a decision. I remembered a recent conversation about lemon chicken so I ordered that. Ten minutes later it was in cardboard containers, the kind without metal handles that you can put in the microwave the next day. 'Lemon chicken?' Courtney said. 'I hate lemon chicken. I told you last week, 'Never order the lemon chicken. It always sucks.' 'Oh,' I said. There didn't seem to be anything else to say."

The narrator continues his story with a reminiscence of the day he left her:

Courtney and I broke up in the bakery. It was just me
and Joseph working that day. He was mixing some rolls
in that careful way he had. Nobody else at the bakery
took the kind of pride he did in his work. Courtney came
over in tears saying she couldn't bear another failed relationship. I said maybe we didn't fail. Maybe there is no
oneness. Maybe we're born alone and we die alone. And
maybe that's okay. She told me to go to hell. Once the
door slammed behind her Joseph came over, looked me
in the eye for just a second and handed me a roll. It was
warm and round and fit exactly in the palm of my hand.

And that was the end of Sarah's story.

The years she spent working with Mariah turned out to be
formative for her as well. When she became an accomplished
writer, she wrote a memoir about the time they spent together,
which she called *December Salmon*. It was among the stories
in the manuscript she was preparing for publication, and was
the only directly autobiographical piece she left. Reading it
after she was gone opened new pages in her life for me, and
brought back the voice I so desperately missed:

December Salmon
by Sarah Rose Horowitz

Some things there are no words for
The way colors form when you blink
into the light

the way waffles appear each morning
for breakfast
how bubbles disappear when touched
and the reassuring rhythm of my head
banging against a wood floor

Labels

Julia was my brother Ben's first baby. When she was born my brother became Father, my mother, Grandma, and I became Auntie. Mariah, his second child, is born fair skinned with a shock of reddish blonde hair. She has red cheeks and my middle name, Rose. She is a colicky baby and her fair skin turns blotchy and red whenever she cries, which is often. I pace up and down with her in my brother's Silicon Valley home declaring that she is a vertical baby, child care worker lingo for babies who prefer to be held with their head up and legs down rather than laid down on a lap. Her tiny lips form into a graceful pout that makes me wonder what she is thinking. Mariah does not wave or respond when we sing to her. She does not respond to her name or play with toys. She says no words. When Mom comes home, Mariah's constant babbling gets louder and more intense; bah bah bah BAH! but she does not wave, run over or even look at Mom. Sometimes she looks into the distance, her mouth shaped into an o, her arms raised, hands flapping like duck bills. Three out of four weeks in a month, Mariah's ears are infected. During those times when she can hear she runs through the house smiling, opening and shutting doors.

My sister, Annie, a nurse, reads me her diagnosis from a
big, blue textbook. "Autism is a rare condition in which a
child has severe problems in communication and behavior
and an inability to relate to people in a normal manner."
The doctors at Stanford agree. "It's like somebody died,"
my brother says to a friend. "All those dreams are can-
celed." His friend listens quietly and says, "You know, Ben,
Mariah's the same little girl you've always known. But ever
since the diagnosis, you've changed. All your expectations
have changed."

In Mariah's backyard, shaded by orange and lemon trees
is a plastic playhouse. Mariah shuts the playhouse door
again and again. I narrate, "Open, shut." Mariah looks me
in the eye and tenses with excitement. She opens and shuts
the door again and again, delighted with the game. She spots
Mom and runs towards the gate. Halfway there she turns to
me and grins.

Work

When my brother calls and asks if I would like a job working with Mariah, I have a very clear and simple thought: this
is a reason to get up in the morning. The Buddhists have an
elegant phrase for it: right livelihood. I recently quit my job
after a co-worker was fired (I felt) unfairly. Though I quit in
a fit of righteousness, I risked very little. This is the kind of
grand gesture that being single and childless allows me. One
day, when things at work were coming to a head, I was
home washing dishes, still in a rage. I pictured the dishes flying out of the cupboards and breaking. The cupboard must

have been slightly open, because a plate did in fact fall out of the cupboard. If this were a novel, I would have to leave this part out. It would not be believable.

I am a childcare worker. At least I have been since I began my working life, sometime in college. Since working with children I remember more and more what it was like to be a child—not the facts of my childhood, but the feelings—the delicious warmth of hearing a story, the words wrapping around us like a quilt, the sharp jolt when playtime was over, the hot shame of being reprimanded. For the past five years, I have worked at several urban schools, all of them wanting. The spaces are always cramped and airless. The yards are small and shoes are required because you never know what you might step on in the sand. I understand animals who refuse to breed.

Behavior

Mariah's lessons take place in her bedroom. Because she hears sounds we don't hear and sees things we can't see she would have a hard time learning in a classroom. A former co-worker once told me that when she started teaching, she heard this constant buzz in her brain. She thought it was all that acid she did as a teenager, but really it was all those tiny, busy voices.

Before we can work at the little plastic table, we have to teach Mariah to sit. She is perpetual motion, flitty and graceful as a salmon swimming. Sometimes Mom and Dad find her outside in the wee hours of the morning, jumping on the trampoline. We lure her to the littler plastic table with bubbles. She learns quickly that if she does what we ask, she will get something she wants. This is basic Behaviorism. It seems strange to sit a child like Mariah, who is constant motion, in a plastic chair but within a month she loves the routine, the structure and clarity. I've read that inner city children living in virtual war zones thrive in classrooms run with almost military efficiency. Some days Mariah loves to show off her new skills. Today isn't one of those days. She puts the shapes in their proper slot in the shape sorter, but she does it through tears. I give her lots of breaks and pink crunchberries (only the crunchberries, she will not eat the white pieces). We are both exhausted when the lesson is over. I bring her into the kitchen, sit her down at the big kitchen table, give her crackers and apple juice. Mariah looks at me, her eyes especially blue today, like the color of unpolluted ocean water, and gently hands me a cracker.

If you had told me years ago that I would be using behaviorism on children, I would not have believed you. When I first learned about it in a high school psychology class I hated it. I thought it was a poor explanation of why we are the way we are. I still think that, but perhaps it explains why we do what we do. Money is at least one of the reasons I work. It allows me to live in an old Victorian in the Mission District of San Francisco. It allows me to sit in cafes and drink foamy, overpriced coffee drinks.

Touch

Touch, says the occupational therapist, evokes two kinds of responses, the touch of a friend or a stranger in a dark alley.

For Mariah, the two are sometimes confused. She screams whenever she is bathed or her hair is brushed. We sit on her blue Mickey Mouse quilt, and I brush her with a soft bristled brush. Then I rub lotion on her, a kind of deep pressure massage. I press her with a pillow, and she giggles with delight. When I sit writing notes later, she plays with my long hair. The privacy I have at the end of the day feels like a gift, to read, and talk to no one. I step onto the train and slip back into my single life like an old pair of slippers. Some days they seem worn and dirty, with holes that leave flesh exposed. Other days, their warm, soft texture is a pure and simple joy.

Imitation

There is one lesson Mariah hates above all others: Imitation. She screams and arches her back. She will not clap or wave on command. Imitation is how most of us typically learn. A poetry teacher in college once remarked that we sleep by imitating the action of sleep. When I was sixteen I decided I wanted to be the kind of person who drank coffee and wrote poetry. I'd never done either before, but I bought a blank book and a cappuccino and have been addicted to both ever since.

Eight months after we begin the waving lesson, Mariah is playing under the covers of her parent's queen sized bed, her curls peeking over the quilt. The lessons for the day are over, and the house is beginning to cool off from the day's heat. I go to say goodbye. For the first time she waves back, casually, effortlessly.

Patience

When she thinks I am not looking, Mariah stands in front of the mirror clapping, imitating all the movements she refused to do earlier. When I tell people what I do for a living, they inevitably say, "Oh, you must be very patient." I do not feel patient, but years of working with children has taught me to act patient. In fact, since working with Mariah I think I am less patient with everyone else. I lose patience when my housemates complain about the weather or the lack of cable TV. The ease with which we all form the words to whine seems to me now, a miracle.

When I was about seven, my family went to the Renaissance Faire, a re-creation of an old English county Faire. I was dressed like Maid Marion in a pointy cap and long dress. I was fascinated by a rope ladder tied at an angle. Men easily five times my weight tried to climb to the top and were flipped onto the mats below. But I tried to climb it again and again, convinced success was just out of reach.

First Words

I dream that Mariah is swinging on a swing and as she swings up she says a clear and full sentence. It disappears as quickly as a soap bubble. I sometimes forget that Mariah doesn't speak. When she is happy she smiles with her entire body. When she is sad she is entirely sad. We've learned a few words in sign language, but she signs faster and more gracefully than I do.

It begins with letters. Grandma and I take Mariah to the Little Farm in Tilden Park where she squeals at the chickens and feeds celery to the sheep. We hear her singing, clear, distinct sounds, "E-i-e-i-o." Sometimes we sit on the floor and play with Mr. Potato Head. She loves slotting his features into their proper places. She flaps his arms and gives him a kiss. I hold out the plastic facial features. "Eye," I say. "Eyes," she says. Her first spontaneous word comes in the middle of a lesson. "Break," a request for freedom.

For the first four years of my life I spoke very little. Because I couldn't hear, my speech developed slowly. When I did speak it wasn't clear. "Bye de gathe," I'd say when I wanted a glass of milk. My parents decoded my speech through trial and error, my father sometimes lifting me up so I could show them what I desired. Once, my brother heard some people speaking French and said, "Oh, they speak Sheish like Sarah."

I was born in London where the damp winters kept my nose running and my ears infected. Each spring new words emerged from my mouth, like robins. A tonsillectomy at four stopped my chronic ear infections. I was still hard of hearing but less so. I learned to listen very carefully. Each year they tested our hearing at school, and each year I failed. Someone from school would call my mother who responded, "We're aware of the problem."

Each year during the Passover seder we talk about four children; one wise, one wicked, one simple, and one who cannot speak at all. Traditionally, the wise child is praised for his questions, for wanting to understand the journey from slavery to freedom remembered on Passover. This year I learn that in the mystical tradition it is the child who cannot speak at all who is praised. This child, the mystics say, understands the story on the deepest level, a level beyond language.

December Salmon

An autism expert talks about salmon. Nature, he says, gives us many variations. Salmon usually swim upstream in spring when the tide levels are optimal. There is a group of salmon though who always swim in December. In a drought year the December salmon are the only ones who survive.

Language

When Mariah wants a bottle or a waffle she sometimes bangs her head on the floor until she gets it. She seems oblivious to the pain. We put Polaroid pictures of a waffle and a bottle on the fridge. One day her bottle picture is lost underneath a pile of papers on the kitchen table. She digs through the pile, finds Mom who is talking to someone in the next room, and hands her the picture.

I begin to think life would be much simpler if the rest of us could exchange pictures. Lately I've been having trouble in taquerias. When I ask for "No sour cream," the no gets lost in the buzz of voices and clink of cervezas. I'm tempted to hand the bored distracted women who wrap the burritos a picture of exactly what I want.

The pop psychologists are always counseling good communication. I tried it with the last guy I dated. Ron and I were neighbors and movie buddies. After the movies, we'd hang out at our local coffee shop talking and laughing. We never talked about turning our friendship romantic, but one night, watching a B movie marathon in his studio apartment, I put my hand on his thigh and his mouth moved towards mine. He had a sweetness, a gentleness I liked, but was obviously still in love with his ex-girlfriend. So I told him what I wanted. He stopped calling. My first love once said to me, "There is no perfect communication. All those books are wrong," and I felt relief like a cool breeze, like other conversations we had where he laughed and said, "exactly."

Raising Voices

Mariah and I are walking home with a bag of French fries. I carry the white bag of fries in one hand and Mariah's hand in the other. "I want to eat fries," Mariah says. "Okay," I say and give her a fry. "I want ten fries," She says. I break a few fries into ten pieces. "I want ten, big fries" she insists, moving her hands out to make the sign for big.

On Halloween I go to a friend's party in Oakland. It's an annual event, and my friend always dresses like a Jack O' lantern which, for some reason is comforting to me. There's a man named Jack who comes to the parties who people consistently avoid, not because he's unlikeable but because he's deaf, and you have to shout and repeat everything you say three times, even the inane, offhand comments. I make a point of talking to Jack. He's dressed as a priest, and I'm dressed as the twelve-step program. I'm wearing a sandwich board with each of the twelve steps written on it. He can't figure out what I'm dressed as but recognizes that our costumed persona have a lot in common (belief in a higher

power, taking a moral inventory). Neither of us knows sign
language well enough to communicate, so we shout at each
other over the '70s music. A deaf person in his own community ceases to be disabled but since we are only partially
deaf we exist awkwardly in both worlds. We argue good-
naturedly about the Israeli-Palestinian conflict. I argue that
Israel is a democracy, and there's value in that system, all
those voices having their say. I argue only partly from conviction. Really, I want the form of the argument, the verbal
joust, each of us taking on an idea, a possibility, like characters at a Halloween party. This habit of arguing both sides
of issues is a legacy from my father who defected from his
Marxist faith and became a Republican around the time of
Ronald Reagan's re-election. He grew up with the doctrine
that we are what society makes us. After political comrades
killed a friend, he could no longer believe this. When he told
my sister that he voted for Reagan she hung up on him, the
kind of grand gesture I have always loved her for. Jack and
I talk for half an hour. I vow that next time I'll bring a pen
and notebook so we won't have to shout.

Sound and Light

When Mariah is tall enough to reach the light switch she
switches it on and off again and again, watching the burst
and extinction of light. Mariah is also in the habit of opening and closing the fridge door, sometimes foraging for food,
sometimes just watching the light. Once, the fridge light goes
out. Mom opens fridge door expecting darkness, but someone has illuminated the fridge with a flashlight. When she

hears music, Mariah smiles and dances. Her speech is clear-
est when she sings a Sesame Street song about a starfish. She
watches her videos over and over until she's memorized every
note, every movement. She begins to act them out. She brings
in props, directs us to march at the appropriate time. There
is a home movie of my siblings and me dancing. There is no
sound but I can still hear the Beatles' "Oh blah di Oh blah
dah" in my head. Annie, who was two at the time, is wearing only a diaper and a tye-dyed t-shirt. This may not in fact
be accurate, but is absolutely true.

It was through music that I fell in love with poetry. When
I was a teenager there were rock musicians who cared as
deeply about words as about the music and they became my
soundtrack. *Think while you dance* was the slogan of the
ska bands I followed, simplistic, but it got at something, that
heady combination of beat and words. I bought a journal
and wrote down phrases that caught my ear, as entranced by
the rhythm as by the meaning.

A few years ago I went to Chicago alone. I visited the Art
Institute, which has an impressive collection of impression-
ist paintings. When I stepped out of the museum I had the
desire, as strong as thirst to exist forever in that impression-
ist light. The museum is built on the lake and I walked along
the water. Used to the ocean, I was surprised how large and
grand the lake seemed. Somewhere downtown I heard a
street musician do an uncannily soulful version of "Can You
Tell Me How to Get to Sesame Street?" I decided then and
there that I wouldn't leave Chicago without hearing some
blues. That evening, I went with some fellow travelers from

the hostel to a tiny blues club. Often when I've been to blues clubs I've been disappointed by the watered down music, but this was a deep, resonant blues, as expansive and richly colored as the lake I'd walked around earlier.

On the days when I'm not working with Mariah I work at a local alternative newspaper where I answer phones and write expanded captions. Work is not quite accurate since it is unpaid. One of the reporters refers to it as their white slavery program. Soon I am writing record reviews. It's a gift and I accept it as such. I love the idea of writing about music but it intimidates me. It's always seemed the province of boys with large record collections and an encyclopedic knowledge of music. I write my first record review, 300 words on the Cure's new record. It is a revelation to me that I can do this without mimicking those boys.

Self-Abuse

Periodically we have to take Mariah to the ear doctor and each time, she tantrums. She thrashes on the ground, bangs her head, and bites herself. Having spent many hours in ear, nose, and throat clinics myself, I think I understand. Mariah's infections are so severe we take her to a specialist. She is strapped onto the examining table without a word. I've had vets give more explanation to my cats. She screams through the entire procedure, which I expect. When it's all over, she's still screaming. White, hot indignation propels me across the room where she sits sobbing. "All done," I say. There's a flicker of recognition in her eyes and then she is quiet. When we are in pain, we hurt ourselves. This is strange but true.

Whenever Joseph and I were together alcohol was involved. Maybe it was because our first night together was spent in a bar, or maybe it was that I sensed the end early; saw something in his eyes looking past me. I met Joseph in my apartment. He drove up to San Francisco from Huntington Beach to visit his sister, my roommate. He had curly black hair, dark framed glasses, and a guitar slung over his shoulder. When he walked into our apartment something in me vibrated and sent out shock waves. Joseph had showed up unannounced and his sister was busy that night so I took him to our neighborhood bar, a funky bar with busts of James Dean, Elvis Presley, and Marilyn Monroe on Grecian pillars. I drank Black Russians and he drank beer. I matched him drink for drink. He stayed a week in which we were inseparable. When we weren't drinking we were laughing or arguing. He always took the conservative point of view partly to get my goat, though I knew he was really arguing with himself, with his hippie heart. Later on in our friendship, we would occasionally reverse roles. We visited the bar several more times that week. After one of our drunken evenings we ended up in bed. We woke up the next morning, arguing. We argued about dialects. He thought they kept people poor and isolated. I thought they enriched the language. Ever after, our meetings were always soaked in alcohol. At some point my stomach started to rebel against coffee, citrus fruits, and alcohol, but I drank anyway. I told myself I didn't mind when Joseph's eyes drifted to other women in the bar. Our evenings ended with me bent over the toilet, hurling. This is not a story about addiction and recovery though. When he wasn't around, I rarely even thought about alcohol. When my heart eventually broke, I ached as if I'd been banging my body against a hard floor.

Out

Recently I met a woman. It's only after meeting her that I understand what a complicated sentence that is: *I met a woman*. She was born with either a very short penis or very large clitoris. In order to save her from locker room trauma, the doctors removed her very large clitoris (or tiny penis), and she has never had an orgasm. She has taken a page from the "out and proud" gay culture in San Francisco and started a support group with T-shirts that say *Hermaphrodites with Attitude*s. When I ask her which gender she identifies with, she says, "both and neither." I am sometimes given to taking political events personally, but the tragedies in Somalia and Bosnia have only left faint traces on my consciousness. It's as if the sheer number of suffering faces prevents any of them from coming into focus. I can't get this woman's story out of my head though. It's the irrevocability that haunts me. What was done to her cannot be undone. Private pleasure has been sacrificed for public normalcy.

It is five in the morning and I am sitting on my bed in my ratty bathrobe, phone to my ear, interviewing a surgeon on the east coast who does surgery on hermaphrodites. "Are you that woman from the *Mercury News*?" he wants to know. "She was up here observing the facilities. She's taking a month off to write her piece. She was terrific." I can hear what he's really saying: *you are just a freelancer for a free weekly. You are not a real journalist.*

My sister-in-law dreams that Mariah is a young woman married to a wealthy man who loves her. She is wearing a red chiffon dress, her hair gracefully swept up on top of her head. She descends a staircase to a party where she is admired for her elegance and elusiveness.

Sometimes I take Mariah to a playground where older children play baseball. She loves to catch the ball though the rules and hand-eye coordination are beyond her right now. I ask the children to play with her, and they indulge me briefly by throwing the ball and letting her chase it. When her part is over, she watches the other children play. At this point she always starts to cry.

We move our classroom out of Mariah's bedroom and go out on the town. We hang out at the Jack-in-the-Box, a taqueria, the library. I ask her questions I know she can answer. "What's your name?" "How old are you?" "What's your favorite food?" Mariah's diet until now consisted mostly of French fries and red grapes. In the Jack-in-the-Box she learns to eat hamburgers, one bite at a time in exchange for a fry. The Silicon Valley suburb where Mariah lives is full of new money, and the schools here boast about their students' high test scores. On good days people see Mariah using sign language and ask me, "Is your daughter deaf?" Once, tired and overheated from the South Bay sun, she tantrums so violently a man follows me in his car, convinced I was kidnapping her. Sometimes Mariah babbles loudly or steals other people's french fries and someone will give me a look, a look that says we have no right to be here. "You think it's hard being black in America?" my brother who is not black says to his wife who is. "Try being Autistic!" Twenty years ago the disabled were kept hidden inside homes and institutions. We take Mariah out so she can get used to crowds, learn to listen with background din, inhabit a public space, but it occurs to me more and more that she isn't the only one changed by this. Slowly, incrementally, I can feel the way her presence demands that public space expand.

Lost

Mariah and I are at the drugstore across the street from her house where we look at toys and buy candy. She bounces down the aisles quickly, and I lose her. Frantic that she'll exit out the front door, I alert the cashier that there's a lost autistic child in the store. "I'll page her," he says. I say, "You don't understand." I find her shortly after, staring lovingly at the candy section.

At five she gets the wanderlust. She figures out how to unlock the front door and take an unescorted walk. We find her at the Jack-in-the-Box eating fries. I like to imagine that she went up to the counter and signed "fries," but this is probably not what happened. I dream that she is lost, only this time we don't find her. In the dream I wake up days after her disappearance, and it hits me that she's really gone. The second time she runs away she is across El Camino at a used car lot marked irresistibly with colored balloons. El Camino stretches across seventy-five miles of the south peninsula. It is essentially a freeway. I try to come up with a rational explanation for her safe crossing, but I can't.

"What I remember about you is that you were always lost," my older brother says, and it's true. When I was three, we visited Harriman State Park in upstate New York. We were by the lake that my parents remember now as being impossibly crowded, when I disappeared. When my father found me I was walking along singing to myself, unaware that I was lost. Two years later we went to the Exploratorium in San Francisco. As we were leaving I paused to look at some mirrors hanging from a ceiling. I no longer remember what was so interesting about the reflection but I remember that it seemed like only a minute had passed before I looked up and everyone was gone. Yesterday, I got lost again, and I was so frustrated I thought I would explode. There were mobs of people—very few were natives or spoke English and the Carol Doda neon was gone—that was my landmark: just look for the light-up tits.

Flying

Mariah is at the end of a long rainbow-colored leash, running around the San Jose airport, me close behind, with french fries and toys. Years ago someone wrote to Dear Abby that seeing children on leashes offended her. "It's a child, not a dog," the writer sniffed. At the time, I think I probably agreed. Now it seems like a kindness to both of us. It keeps her safe. We board first, before "others with small children or people needing assistance." As we rise I feel my ears pop. Mariah cries at just that moment, and I know that her ears must be popping too. "Do your ears hurt?" I ask, pointing to my ears. She stops crying and looks at me, her eyes relieved that she has been understood. I regret that this is all I can do.

When we arrive at my father's house in Los Angeles, I show Mariah the bathroom, but she doesn't go. Although she's potty trained, she won't always go in strange toilets. It's a temperate Los Angeles, December day, we walk to the park. Mariah walks between us, Grandpa and I each holding a hand. "1, 2, 3," we chant, then lift her so she is flying, legs tucked under, arms out. We count again, "One, two..." a smaller, higher voice finishes. "Three, she says, grinning at me. She grins again when she's swinging on the swing. "Push," she says, and I push her. She is soaring over the trees, and I remember that feeling of swinging, taking off, watching the sky continually appear and disappear. The empty swing next to her invites me, and I swing next to her. She laughs, a genuine laugh, the laugh of a preschooler who knows that grown-ups swinging is funny. She jumps off the swing, and gives me gentle pushes so I'll go higher. Walking home from the park she spots a Taco Bell sign. Ecstatic to see a familiar landmark, she smiles and signs taco. I think how strange it must be for her to wake up in a strange place, what extraordinary trust it took for her.

I'm standing at the stove, stirring macaroni and cheese when I feel a weight on my legs. They are being wrapped in a bear hug. Later, we all eat at the dining room table. While we are eating, the phone rings, and I take the call in the kitchen. When I return, Grandpa tells me that Mariah didn't eat a bite while I was gone. She finally goes to the bathroom that evening, and I breathe a sigh of relief. I lie down on the double bed with her, afraid she'll have one of her bouts of insomnia. After rolling around and giggling for a while she sleeps through the night. She wakes up the next morning smiling at the mirror next to our bed. On the plane going home I sing "Old Macdonald" (Mariah supplies the animal sounds). She steals a muffin from the elderly lady next to me who gives me a wicked look. Mariah runs ahead when we deplane, her rainbow leash trailing behind her, me at the other end.

Obsession

Mariah has a number of obsessions; videos, dogs, food. We taught her to crack eggs and stir. Once, mom made a pie for her sister, Julia. She set it down on the kitchen table to cool and found it five minutes later, covered in salt. She made a second pie, put it on top of the fridge. Again, she found the pie on the kitchen table, covered in salt, a chair strategically placed in front of the fridge.

It's letters that are her most enduring obsession. Mariah loves letters with the passion of a ten-year-old baseball fan. When she is not jumping on the trampoline she is usually looking at books. She moves my finger across her wooden alphabet puzzle and sings the alphabet song. It took her a matter of weeks to learn their names. When we go out on walks now, she notices license plates. We read Dr. Seuss's *ABC* book over and over. Letters were her first clear speech. The letters are starting to form words for her. We remove the pictures from the fridge and replace them with words. She stands there studying them with a reverence I understand.

"As soon as you figured out that you could put letters together and form words you were hooked," my mother says. I don't remember a time before words, before stories. I can remember what I was reading as vividly as I can my friends from any given year. A childhood friend remembers that I would often stop whatever game we were playing and say, "Okay, let's read." I can read walking down the street, by candlelight, even in a moving car. If I'm not reading I feel slightly unhinged. Once, during a time in my life when money was scarce, I spent money on a hardback book. "It was a book emergency," I told my mother sheepishly. I read about a study that found that in marriages that lasted, couples continued to tell each other the story of how they met and fell in love.

Following my obsession has led me here, to a bar where anyone can read their poetry on Sunday nights, the Paradise Lounge. I have been planning to read for months, but each week I decide my poetry is not good enough, I am too shy to get up in front of all these people, I will not read this week. So I'm not sure how I got here, standing on stage, behind a microphone, in front of an abstract painting full of grey-blues and yellows. I read a poem about Mariah. As I read, the words take on weight, a solidity the texture of photographs.

Ritual

The pre-school children sit in a circle, sing or listen to stories. Mariah does not join them. She stands outside the circle.

When the children talk about the month and the days of the week, they count. Mariah turns, and her face fills with light. The counting delights and comforts her. She is intent, as if in prayer. Each morning I sit and sip coffee, listening to my breath, and watch the steam rise from my cup. Friday evenings I light candles and watch the flames flicker. On Saturday morning I wrap myself in my grandfather's silk tallis and go to *shul* where we chant the same liturgy each week and tell the same stories again and again. On weeks when I don't do this, I feel as if I have stumbled and lost my balance.

My hearing has been quickly dimming. I can hear almost nothing without the aid of batteries now. My hip, too, is deteriorating. I begin to imagine myself inhabiting a smaller and smaller space without movement or voices. The day I turn thirty-six, I arrive at the *shul* to meet my rabbi. We enter the empty sanctuary together. The chill surprises me like linoleum on bare feet. The light is filtered like dust through the colored glass of the windows. We open the imposing ark, each of us holding open a heavy, wooden door. Inside the ark is the velvet-encased Torah. I place a pillbox with pain killers, a cup of water, and my hearing aid in the ark. We read *Shema Koleinu*, a prayer that begins with the word "Listen."

"When our strength is gone, do not abandon us," we read. I take my pills and attach my hearing aid to my ear as I do each morning. I resent and rely on these things. When I first heard the rabbi speak he talked about Camus and Torah, wove words around words and enveloped me. He places his hands on my head and recites *El Malei*

Rachamim, a prayer traditionally said for mourners. There is a powerful emptiness in the room like a sigh or a strong wind.

Days later I dream that I am going to work but there is a huge fire on the way. I can't get past the people and the fire trucks. It is too dangerous and difficult to navigate. Wooden boards are being hurled off the roof. A woman tells me someone has just been shot. I am distressed that I can't get where I am going until it hits me that I am not going to the fearful place I think I'm going. In this week's Torah portion the Israelites are at the edge of the Sea of Reeds and see the Egyptian soldiers. Though the Israelites outnumber the Egyptians, they are afraid. Moses instructs them to stand still and collect themselves so they do. They enter the water, the sea parts improbably and they cross, like December salmon.

Winter

Annie Sprinkle says that too many women starve waiting for gourmet sex. I vow to have more junk-food sex, or at least pizza sex. D. is the kind of guy who asks you how you are so he can tell you how he is. It seems like the perfect relationship for the 90's, down-sized expectations and all. "You're so quiet," he'd say, but really it was hard to get a word in edgewise. He was afraid I would get too attached, but I was already turning off. The work I have done for three years is ending too. Mariah is starting school, and the paper I write for has been sold. Everyone is in cubicles now, and most of my co-workers have been fired. I remember when we watched the presidential debate together, seduced momentarily by Clinton's words. Now I am standing in the rain, reading that the Democrats no longer hold the House. Newt Gingrich and his cronies are marching into office. It's been raining hard and constantly for weeks. The weather forecasts are predicting a cold winter.

Emotion

It's been three years since I've worked with Mariah, though I visit. She always asks to take a walk. We walk in silence, enjoying each other's company. We go ice skating at the mall, but this interests her only briefly. She is eight now, taller and heavier than the last time we went skating and is unsure how to navigate her new body. I'm always shocked by how tall and muscular she is. In my imagination she is still wiry and thin. "Pizza," she says, spotting a pizza sign. I take her to Chuck E. Cheese, a place I find over-stimulating but Mariah loves. There are grotesque, overstuffed animals and endless games. Mariah shows me her favorite, whack-a-mole. I watch her eat pizza and marvel that she once lived on french fries and red grapes. She asks for something, but I don't understand. She grabs a pen and writes "farm." She is remembering the little farm in Tilden Park we used to go to. We go home, sit on the couch and watch Barney videos. Although her musical repertoire now includes hipper fare like Britney Spears she's still fond of the purple dinosaur. She turns to me and smiles. "Happy," she says.

6

Love Turns Pain
into Medicine

When Sarah settled into the new apartment on Bush Street, she became master of her own space and began to move in new directions. "She wanted to be a different person, wanted a new life," Emily recalls. "She loved living by herself, without roommates; it gave her a new independence. Whatever she did now didn't involve socially who she was living with, and this allowed her to really define herself and in particular to embark on her religious path."

The year after the move a friend introduced her to Congregation Beth Sholom in San Francisco's Richmond District, and not long afterwards she joined. It was the first time she had attended a *shul* regularly since her *Bat Mitzvah* twenty years before. Emily had recently undergone a conversion to Judaism and had seen Sarah's engagement coming for a long time. When they were roommates, they had prepared Passover dinners regularly, and Emily felt that

"Sarah always craved some connection with Judiasm that was appropriate for her and in line with her beliefs." Judaism provided an added attraction in the fact that "it is the only religion where being a good writer and a good reader are important and that's what Sarah was about. So it was a perfect marriage."

The congregation she had found was progressive, allowing women to be full participants in the services, but was also conservative in its attitude towards the liturgy. In it she encountered individuals who were socially open-minded and intellectual, and who were serious about their faith. The group also had an unusual spiritual guide who seemed perfectly suited to Sarah's needs.

Rabbi Alan Lew was nearly my age and had been brought up in a liberal household in Brooklyn. His parents were secular Jews who identified with the recently created state of Israel, but his grandfather was a rabbi whom he often accompanied as a young boy to *shul*. After his graduation from college, Lew moved to California where he became part of the "New Age" movement, which was embracing eastern religions. He settled in Berkeley, became a poet and a Zen Buddhist, and embarked on a path to become an ordained monk. One day, however, in the course of his spiritual training, he realized that he could not complete the conversion because he was unable to bring himself to say the words required—*I take refuge in the Buddha.*

"I couldn't say it," he explained in a memoir he wrote, "because I was a Jew. The problem wasn't that I felt I was betraying God. In fact when I was sitting in *zazen* [meditation], I often felt more in contact with God than I ever had before. But I felt I was betraying my soul. Mine was a Jewish soul. I was betraying myself." Lew went back to New York and enrolled in the Jewish Theological Seminary to become a rabbi like his grandfather. In pursuing Judaism, he decided to incorporate the meditation techniques and insights he had absorbed from his Buddhist practice. By the time Sarah joined his congregation, he was widely known as the Zen Rabbi.

Initially, the relationship between them wasn't as close as it eventually became. "At first, Rabbi Lew didn't 'get' her," says Henry Hollander, a member of the congregation who, along with his wife Katherine, was to become one of Sarah's closest friends. "He would answer a question she posed, and she wouldn't come back at him with a response immediately, the way other people did. But as time passed, he came to respect her so much that he was probably afraid to disappoint her. Sarah was a person who walked the walk and became frustrated with people who did not. She believed very strongly in traditional Judaism and in egalitarian Judaism, both of which Rabbi Lew pushed against some resistance in the congregation. As the community's leader, he was inevitably subject to pressures from both sides. If Rabbi Lew yielded too much ground on the principles he espoused, there were people with whom it might go unnoticed. But Sarah would notice. He came to appreciate Sarah quite deeply after awhile. He was aware that she was as good a critical reader of what he had to say and what he had to do as he was likely to get, and as a result he paid attention."

Sarah embraced Rabbi Lew's fusion of two spiritual worlds, which was clearly in keeping with her lifelong quest to build bridges that brought people together. "She liked the two of them," observes Emily, "*Halacha* in Judaism and Right Mindfulness in Buddhism. *Halacha* is the Jewish law, the path or the process of negotiating justice in the world. There's a natural affinity between *Halacha* and the Buddhist idea of Right Mindfulness." Sarah also liked the concept and practice of meditation. "She liked the idea that there was something bigger than the self. She liked not being materialistic, not being attached to things, and being mindful about everything she did. She liked there to be a reason for what she did."

A few years after Sarah first joined the congregation, Rabbi Lew began a meditation group called *Makor Or*, or "Source of Light." Sarah was a charter member. In a notebook which she named "My Practice," she charted the progress of her spiritual path:

January 9—On my birthday (thirty-six, double *chai*) R. Lew and I did a ritual. We said *Shema Koleinu* which says "Hear our voice, don't abandon us in our frailty." Then I took my Tylenol and put on my hearing aid. It acknowledged the loss of my hip and hearing and also where my help comes from. We both felt palpably the presence of the *shechina* [holy spirit] hovering over us. R. Lew was so moved he spontaneously placed his hands on my head and said *El Molei Rachamim*. "I have a feeling you're going to get an answer," he said.

As she continued the entry in her practice book, she set down her innermost fears, which she had never confided in me or her mother:

And then I had a dream. The dream said I am not going to the scary place I think I'm going. At least I hope that's what it said. I really was scared of going to this place where I can't move and can't hear. And then the next week's *parshah* was about how the Israelites saw "*tsar mitzrayim*" the spirit of Egypt and were afraid out of proportion to the situation. So they stood still. And they jumped into the sea. And the sea parted.

The sessions with Rabbi Lew buoyed her spirits and began an introspective journey that would lead her out of the slough of frustration and anxiety that at times threatened to engulf her. The exhilaration of the discipline she had undertaken and the self-discovery it brought was already evident in her next entry:

January 30—Splendid day yesterday—meditation, prayer, dancing—I'm such a *yutz* but I don't care. The music and the dancing are so beautiful. And my body felt so good afterwards, awake—a perfect Sunday. I'm struck by how the daily practice really transforms the whole day, in a quiet subtle way. It transforms prayer too. I'm aware of this powerful sense that all the souls that prayed before us are there.

The next day she was scheduled to meet with Rabbi Lew, and she took time to set down in her practice book the things she wanted to take up with him. She also described the impact of the sessions she had already completed. "When I meditate," she wrote, "I feel this very powerful sense that I am exactly who I am supposed to be, exactly where I am supposed to be."

This was the goal—self-understanding and acceptance. But once she left the meditation sessions and stepped back into the "real world," she found it difficult to hold onto the resolution she had achieved. In reflection, she was able to identify three specific feelings that surfaced during the meditations, which she thought were probably the same ones that distracted her in the rest of her life. The feelings were "anger, anxiety, and social anxiety," and she made a note to discuss them with Rabbi Lew at their meeting.

January 31—Met with R. Lew today. Asked him about feeling like I am exactly who I am supposed to be, exactly where I'm supposed to be, doing exactly what I'm supposed to be doing. He said he was really thunderstruck by my question because when I walked in he thought, "Sarah is exactly who she is supposed to be...." Not sure if that is literally true, but I feel that he believes that about me. I'm still wondering if I 'did it right.' Was I supposed to start talking first? Did I say stupid things? But whatever I did, it didn't ruin it. The depth, the warmth of the communication: Wow.

At the same time she was engaged in her spiritual work with Rabbi Lew, she was enrolled in the Masters of Fine Arts program at the University of San Francisco. When she broached these studies with Lew, she had already been in the program six months, working to complete her long unfinished novel. She talked to Lew about her feelings of inadequacy in confronting the challenge she had set for herself. The first school term had just ended, and she was discouraged enough to confide in Emily that she thought she was going to flunk out. In the session with Lew, she brought up her feelings in a more guarded way: "I told Rabbi Lew I was anxious about doing well in school. In his guru officious way he said, 'You are doing well in school.' Tonight I found out I got a merit scholarship for spring semester." It was a revelation of the gap between her self-perception and her reality.

Among the anxieties she confided to Lew were her feelings about being alone, and not finding a life partner. A few weeks after this entry, she wrote in her notes: "You are not fear or unworthiness. Those are just feelings you sometimes have." In another session, she tried to persuade him that her resistance to the praise she received for her writing was a "spiritual issue and not a matter of low self-esteem." Lew was not impressed and told her that she did, in fact, have low self-esteem and she had to work on that. "He also said my fear of meditation's power is a fearing my own power."

These conversations were high points in her journey but also, inevitably, occasions for renewed self-doubt. "It's so exciting to have someone to talk to, someone wizened as well as open. I wonder if this is a waste of his time. I do always assume I'll fail, and it isn't always counter-intuitive to think so. But he's right. It's a bad habit, the habit of failure. I think I just have to live it out, breathe out the anxiety, the feelings of unworthiness. So much easier said than done."

But she was doing it, and getting constant rewards for her efforts: "The world looked so beautiful this morning after I left *Makor Or*. There were brilliant patches of light peeking through the morning sky. I feel a heightened sense of beauty which is not at all aesthetic because I'm sitting in a butt ugly cafeteria. I don't think it's sleep deprivation either. There's the same dreamy quality but this feels like my awareness is keener not dulled."

Not all her issues were spiritual. She was dieting and had begun to lose weight. In her notebook, she recorded her pleasure at the achievement, along with her bouts of backsliding: "Wow. I just ate fettucine alfredo (small portion) followed by a cookie. I won't think too hard about it. I am really hungry. I don't want to gain that weight back though. I feel so much lighter, so much more attractive (much as I hate admitting that)."

Another participant in the *Makor Or* sessions was Rabbi Lew's friend Norman Fischer. The two had met when both attended the University of Iowa's writer's workshop in the 1960s. A Buddhist priest and poet, and former abbot of the

San Francisco Zen center, Fischer formed a strong bond with Sarah.

> *March 4*—Norman said something that really stayed with me, about approaching suffering as if it is temporary, so that there is a constant letting go. It made sense to me because when I'm really suffering it's when I have this consciousness of becoming deafer and deafer, more and more crippled, in that small place, isolated and immobile.

Once again she noted her difficulty in maintaining the clarity she had achieved once she left the sessions. "Letting go makes perfect sense to me inside meditation. What I'm not sure of is how to translate that to real life, or ordinary life. In ordinary life, in habit—fear, anxiety, frustration, and anger."

These feelings came together as the focus of one of her most vivid and revealing notes:

> Woke up this morning and went into a rage because my ear amp was feeding back. Caught myself quickly but it brought home how much anger there is around physical crap (also brought home that I am sleep deprived). Went to meditation, or got on the bus to go anyway, and when I got to my stop I got off and saw that the light on Geary was green already so I waited because I can't run anymore. I just can't do it. The bus driver actually re-opened the bus doors to tell me to cross. What is it, his

business? It enraged me.

And then she wrote:

I feel sometimes that the whole universe thinks I'm too slow, and I am slow. I walk slow. I hear slow. I even think slow.

And then:

I was sitting in meditation thinking about this, trying to breathe it out, stay with my breath, but I kept coming back to it, thinking about what I would say to Norman about all this, when suddenly I saw him in my mind and heard his voice very clearly say: *"Sarah, you're the one who's impatient with yourself."*

Norman prescribed a Buddhist practice to reinforce what she had seen. He instructed Sarah to have a "big mind" in her day-to-day life, to observe her anger and frustration. And to let it go.

In another journal entry she recorded her efforts to follow the path he had laid out for her: "I am practicing saying, 'Oh, there's pain again,' or 'I am having trouble hearing again.'" Fischer's counsel about the practice struck yet another chord: "No one has ever said that to me. Not just that spiritual practice in general is a good idea, but that it's a good idea for *me*. Not only do I feel in meditation that I am exactly who I am supposed to be, exactly where I am supposed to be, doing exactly what I am supposed to do, but my fellow meditators see me this way too. This is truly *chein* [beauty], gratuitous grace."

The effect of the practice was to enable her to look at her frustrations with what she described as "a meditative consciousness." It turned her vision around and made her focus on what she had rather than what she didn't. She found herself becoming "more grateful for the moments when I can walk or hear, and no longer take those abilities for granted." In her next consultation with Rabbi Lew, he talked to her about how she might achieve detachment from being deaf and immobile. "He suggested meditating on what the condition is, what I'm hearing, how I'm walking. He said Degas lost his vision in his later years and that the pictures he painted then of what he was seeing were some of his most extraordinary."

This conversation made Sarah reflect on something she had read in a book by the physician Oliver Sachs. It was about an artist who had lost his ability to see color. "At first he tried to paint from memory, but it didn't work, and then he began painting what he saw now and the paintings were wonderful." She reflected on how this might apply to her own case. "At first all I could think was absence, what I *wasn't* hearing. Then I remembered being at summer camp and listening to other girls whispering. I couldn't hear the content, but I could hear the shape, the music. Maybe that's how I fell in love with the music of language. It struck me that this is the way we hear language when we *daven* and pray."

She was now five months into her training, and she was feeling its impact throughout her day. "Rabbi Lew said in *shul* today that we all feel uniquely disabled. He said that when you see someone the way they really are, made in the image of G-d, this is healing. Do I quote him too much? This is why sitting with him and Norman is so powerful." When her conversations with them took place she felt "bathed in kindness." "They make me feel so good about myself I almost feel guilty. It's a love fest. I quote them. They validate me. I joke, but I need that. I forget every day that I am exactly who I'm supposed to be. I'm very glad those two men exist. Rabbi Lew said that I'm a good practice for others. I force them to slow down. HA!"

I cannot begin to describe how happy I am reading these words, which come to me from a past I cannot recover. How they cause me to regret my impatience when we talked on the phone about her novel so many years before; how I wish I could have the words I spoke back; and how grateful I am to these two strangers for coming so forcefully and so wisely into her life as angels of mercy to relieve her distress.

Months after Sarah made the journal entry she revisited her romantic relationship with Joel, and observed how her attitude towards him had changed as well.

This morning during meditation I breathed in all of social anxiety and self-consciousness, and breathed out the love and affection I feel from Rabbi Lew, Norman, and Joel. I was thinking of Joel because of the sweet, sweet note he sent yesterday. But he belongs in this trio anyway because he's always been there to remind me of the best things about me, that, in his words I am 'the bomb.' It's quite amazing actually considering he broke my heart and everything. I still feel a gap between how I am able to see myself the rest of the time versus how I see myself in the presence of these men. Anyway I started crying in meditation. It was the blessings that made me cry, breathing in the love and affection of these men.

That very week I called to tell her about a dream I had about her, which had caused me to bolt awake in the night in an anxious sweat. She recorded the dream in her notebook where I found it after she was gone. In my fantasy, she was on a mission to Germany where I knew she was going to be killed, but also knew that I couldn't stop her. She told me she had lost her passport, and I had signed the papers that allowed her to go. I was upset because she had an Apple computer, and I was only familiar with PCs and didn't know how to get the information out, and now that she was gone couldn't ask her. But since it was a dream I could speak to her. "What should I do with your writing?" I asked her. And she said: "I have passed on into the world of words. An audience is irrelevant."

Sarah wrote in her notebook: "I love this dream. It's so much about parental anxiety and letting go and also the tremendous transformation I'm going through that he must have picked up on."

During this period in her life, Sarah came down periodically to visit April and me in our Malibu house overlooking the ocean. On these occasions, she liked to curl up in the corner of one of our sofas and read a book she had brought—the latest family novel by Anne Tyler or one of the big volumes from Taylor Branch's biography of Martin Luther King. April would bring her some tea, and she would cup her small hands around the bowl to warm them, and then return to her reading.

In the breaks she took from her text, one of us would sit down beside her to talk. When it was my turn, she would quiz me about events that happened in the Sixties or about my parents' generation and the Old Left. I gave her a book called *The Romance of American Communism* to read, and we discussed it. She had a natural curiosity about my experiences, but I understood she was also researching backgrounds for the stories she was writing. When April was alone with her, they would talk about personal things, about her relations with her siblings, and her love life. She told April she would like to be married and have a family, but she didn't currently have any prospect and, because of her condition, couldn't have any children. "Are you happy?" April asked her. "Yes," she answered, and there was no doubting she was.

Two years after she began her meditations, her aunt Barbara collapsed in the New York apartment where she lived alone, the victim of a fatal aneurysm. As the first anniversary of her death approached, Sarah noted in her journal:

It's been a year of loss and sitting with that loss. I have a new respect for the awesome power of the practice.

Just sitting with loss (and fear) was so liberating...and empowering. I'm not sure what else to say about this. Am I closer to discovering my divine name? [This was a challenge Rabbi Lew had given her.] Not sure. Really not sure. Living with uncertainty. Being willing to go down the rabbit hole. I sat between Norman and Rabbi Lew today, and the image of being sheltered, protected, kept rising up. I thought of my dear friends Henry and Katherine, and everyone at *Makor Or* and their sheltering love. It's a-rational. I am not sheltered from ordinary and probably not even extraordinary suffering. Yet there it is. "The children of God were saved, but they were not safe." I still feel Barbara's love though she is gone. Save, Savor, Cherish.

The observance of the holiday *Tisha B'av* occurs on the 9th day of the month of Av. It is a dark memorial for Jews, commemorating the destruction of the Temple in Jerusalem by the Babylonians in 586 BCE and again, on the same date, by the Romans in 70 CE. It is one of the only religious observances during which Jews are allowed to write, and Sarah resolved to make it a day on which she would put down her thoughts. Just before the anniversary of her aunt's death, she wrote: "Structures that have fallen this year— that all the love I have for Barbara would have no place to go, and I would no longer be able to feel her love." It was Rabbi Lew's counsel: *Pay attention to the ways in which the relationship continues.*

She went on with her soliloquy, turning inward:

The major problem in my life is lack of romantic inti-
macy. The major problem with myself is I'm too slow.
There is a way in which relationships continue after
death or separation. My life will be no more bereft without a partner than with. The desire is the fulfillment.
Every day I miss those I have loved. But also every day I
appreciate utterly and completely being single. I think
slow, walk slow, hear slow, was late to get my advanced
degrees and whatever else. But it feels now like just my
rhythm. And I think it's allowed me to enjoy ageing in a
manner that few others can. I have come into my own in
so many ways.

At Sarah's funeral, Rabbi Lew read a verse by the Sufi
poet Rumi, who had written one of the lines Sarah cherished
most. In her notebook Sarah said of these words: "This is
my mantra. I had no idea I was going to be so crippled and
deaf but I was at exactly the right place when it happened.
My community of friends buoyed me up yesterday in amazing, amazing ways."

Rumi's verse and Sarah's mantra was this: "Love turns
pain into medicine."

7

Her Divine Name

Before she joined Beth Sholom and met Rabbi Lew, Sarah had participated in the causes of the Left, but as a supporter not an activist. She was a frequent marcher in anti-war demonstrations and a writer of letters in behalf of political prisoners. But she was never an ideologue. "Even when we were younger," Emily observes, "she was a thoughtful person, never a party liner. She was for peace and justice but knew when things were not right in the positions and behaviors of the left. A lot of that had to do with what she learned from you about that, about philosophies that were all-encompassing and positions that didn't make sense. The older we got it became clearer and clearer that the left was not our friend a lot of the time, particularly on Israel."

Sarah explained her involvement in social causes this way:

When I was growing up my father was a devout Marxist. My mother volunteered in the schools and noticed that many of the children were coming to school hungry, so my father helped the Black Panther Party with its free school breakfast programs. Later, my father was embittered by the many murders justified by Marxist ideology. This left me with a two-fold legacy. I have always felt driven to pursue justice, but am wary of ideology and partisan politics.

Sarah then described the spiritual dimension of her commitments to social causes: "While I became very good at arguing against the death penalty from a practical point of view, I realized that there was a deeper, spiritual foundation for my opposition. I realized that what I really wanted to say is that it's bad for the soul of the nation. And there's no real traditional political language for that—the collective soul. At some point, I read an amazing sermon by Martin Luther King, which he wrote right after the Montgomery bus boycott. Basically he said don't get on the bus full of braggadocio, because you still have to live with these people. And I kind of realized that that was the sort of political action that I wanted to be a part of. I wanted to recognize the dignity of living. I started exploring synagogues, and then I was very lucky to connect with Rabbi Alan Lew who articulated a Jewish vision of social justice that resonated deeply with me."

Sarah was aware of the problems inherent in attempts to apply religious ambitions to social changes, and was cautious about that, too. "A lot of what is going on now in our country around combining religion and politics is actually very dangerous," she wrote. "Religion is not about 'God wants you to vote for the Green Party.' In my mind, it's more about the way in which you fight the battle."

Her spiritual approach to social concerns was strongly influenced by her new teacher. "Meditation and Jewish practice lead us to experience the oneness of all beings," Lew wrote in his autobiography, which he called *One God Clapping*. "We are all connected; each of us is created in the divine image, and other people's suffering is our own. Therefore, we have no choice but to try to heal it." In a parallel vein, Sarah wrote: "At the heart of Judaism is Abraham's vision of oneness, the idea that we're all deeply connected. I think that is at the heart of things for those of us who pursue social justice."

Among the causes inspired by this vision and championed by Rabbi Lew was the plight of the homeless. Lew led demonstrations in their behalf and on one occasion was arrested for his efforts. On the back of a manuscript page she left behind, Sarah had scrawled in long hand a description of her commitment to this cause:

Once, in a protest put on by Religious Witness With The Homeless, the names of all those who had died that year on San Francisco's streets were read, a simple yet powerful act that says 'you are known.' And I felt something I rarely feel at staged events like this—true grief for the simple acts of love for these who had too little of in life:

clothing, food and shelter. When I lived in the Mission, I gave spare change freely to my homeless neighbors. Years after I'd moved to the Richmond, I rode the bus with a woman who remembered that I used to give her change in front of the Rainbow Grocery. I had not recognized her because she was completely transformed. She had found a job and a place to live. Not everyone has the capacity to transform their lives as this woman did, but I believe we all remember those who clothed us when we were cold.

Another cause that resonated with Sarah was the campaign to abolish the death penalty. Whenever there was an execution at San Quentin, Rabbi Lew led members of his congregation on vigils at the site, and Sarah was there with him. The vigils frequently had to be held in the dead of winter when the approaches to the prison were exposed to the Bay winds, and the bone-snapping cold. Sarah wrote a story about these vigils which showed once again how closely she incorporated her own life and its ambivalences into her art. She called her fiction, "Two, Three, Many Vietnams," which was a slogan invented by the Cuban Marxist Che Guevara, intending to ignite a global conflagration. When I was a radical, I had used the same slogan as the title of a book I edited for *Ramparts*. But in Sarah's story the words were given an entirely new meaning.

Her main character was a journalist named Chaim, who had come to San Quentin to report on an execution. "Chaim" is the Hebrew word for life. Sarah's story begins:

"Vietnam was the dividing line for his generation Chaim thought, as he marched in darkness towards San Quentin, a tiny sliver of a moon hanging over the blue-black water. Where you'd stood on that war defined you in a way no other issue did." To underscore the point she was making, she added, "When his best friend had quit AA and started hanging out in bars again Chaim had said, 'This will be your Vietnam.'"

The character, Chaim, is described as a one-time anti-war leftist who was "an angry and idealistic student at San Francisco State...staunchly against the war, horrified by the Mai Lai massacre, the napalm, and his government's lies." The San Quentin prisoner whose execution is about to take place is "a veteran from the war Chaim had marched against." Some of Chaim's friends are activists who had second thoughts about their radical protests, "who still considered themselves on the left though they mostly voted Republican now, because of their position on that war over thirty years ago." Sarah describes one of them as "losing faith in the left...dismayed by the carnage of the Communist peace," and by "the Left's silence" over the millions of Cambodians and Vietnamese the Communists killed after they took power.

These were themes of my own writings, and the friend that is mentioned is a fictional representation of Ronald Radosh, a radical whom I have known for more than fifty years, and whose views I had discussed with Sarah. In her story, Sarah describes him as someone who "couldn't seem to let go of the idea himself as a man of the Left," which is exactly how had I described Ron to her. Ron was also an avid admirer of the folk music and protest songs of the Sixties, and couldn't imagine being separated from them. In Sarah's story the Radosh character laments that what he will miss most about the Sixties is the music. "Chaim knew what he meant. Where had that vision, that hope gone? That flash in the gut you got after listening to Dylan that a better world was just out of reach?"

When Chaim arrives at San Quentin, a crowd of protesters has already gathered outside the prison walls. The Buddhist monks among them are meditating and the native Americans are banging drums. Other activists are chanting "Ho hey, hey ho, capital punishment's got to go." The narrator explains to the reader that the Buddhist monks had begun coming to the vigils when one of their own was executed after being convicted on "hazy" evidence. The native Americans first joined the protests we are told "as the final request of a Native American man who'd tortured and murdered several women." But in his case there are no ambiguous facts.

The Vietnam veteran scheduled to be executed that night was suffering from post-traumatic stress syndrome and was not in his right mind. Those who knew him said that he came back from Vietnam "a different and broken man," haunted by the war. He was convicted of murdering a 70-year-old woman who was watching a war movie on television. "He'd heard the sound of gunfire, broke into her home, killed her and, like a good soldier, tagged her toe."

This was a true story. The name of the condemned man was Manny Babbitt, whose execution was the first Sarah attended. She had made his case the focus of a *drash*—one of the sermons that members of the congregation were often asked to give during services at Beth Sholom. *Drash* is the term for a commentary on the Sabbath text and is always a passage taken from the first five books of the Old Testament, which tell the story of the Jews from the creation of the world until their entry into the promised land. The *drash* in which Sarah mentioned Manny Babbitt was an exegesis of the Torah portion "Pinchas," about a biblical figure who executed two individuals for participating in forbidden sex rites.

The interesting element in the passage was that God had made the executioner a *Kohen* or priest after the deed. This raised many questions and inspired many commentaries. Why would God honor a man who had committed such acts? In providing an answer Sarah noted that several commentators had interpreted the honor God accorded Pinchas "not as a reward for his extremism but as a kind of healing. The *K'tav sofer* says that 'He will have to cure himself of his violent temper if he is to function as a *Kohen*.' Hamek Davar says, 'This will protect Pinchas from the destructive impulse within him.'" Sarah also cites commentaries from the *Eitz Chaim*, a book provided for the Sabbath services whose title means *Tree of Life*: "The commentators of *Eitz Chaim* note that a person is never the same after he has shed blood, no matter how justifiable the cause."

Manny's brother Bill Babbit spoke at the vigil that Sarah attended at San Quentin and told his story. Bill had turned his own brother into the authorities after being promised they would not try him for a capital offense. When the authorities went back on their word and convicted Manny and sentenced him to death, Bill felt betrayed. Sarah wrote: "Now Babbitt's brother speaks at each execution, trying to save others from his fate. Manny's brother was only indirectly responsible for his brother's death, but I don't think he has ever been the same."

In Sarah's fictional account, Chaim is inspired by the case of Manny Babbitt to the following thought: "When someone died you could see the shape of their life. When someone was executed you saw the shape of a culture."

At this point in the story, Sarah expands her canvas and broadens its themes. As Manny's execution is completed, the crowd grows silent. Deep in his own thoughts, Chaim is reminded of an interview he once conducted with Henry Kissinger, who was America's Secretary of State during the Vietnam War, and whom many leftists regard as a war criminal. Sarah imagines that Chaim's interview with Kissinger took place after he had retired, and was "an old man losing his hearing." During the interview, Kissinger is unrepentant and shows no remorse over the war. When the interview is over, Chaim turns off his tape recorder and asks one final question: What would have happened if the United States had not attempted to prevent Vietnam from falling to the Communists?

"'Wouldn't have mattered very much,' Kissinger muttered. 'If the Vietnam domino had fallen then, no great loss.'" Kissinger's words shock Chaim, who becomes angry and begins mentally to count up the casualties of the war. As he does so, his anger continues to mount and his thoughts turn dark. "For a moment, Chaim fantasized what it would be like to push Kissinger out the window. It would be so easy, just a shove. They were 26 floors up. Chaim's rage became an unbearable pressure. His blood quickened: 'Do it, do it.'"

But Chaim does not "do it." He refuses to take the life, even though he believes Kissinger is criminally responsible for many thousands of deaths that made no difference. "Chaim leaned forward, Kissinger was right there, just across the desk. He bit his lip, hard. A thin line of blood trickled down his chin."

That is the end of Sarah's story. Chaim will not take another life. It is a powerful moral tale even if one doesn't accept its assumption that there would have been no consequences if America had not attempted to prevent a Communist victory in Vietnam. The moral complexity of Sarah's story will not please every reader, but it expresses artfully the unresolved and insoluble dilemmas we all face.

In 1998, the year she joined Beth Sholom, Sarah moved from the Bush Street address to her last apartment on Anza about a mile from the *shul*. The neighborhood was largely made up of Asian and Russian immigrants, and was clean, safe, and comfortingly middle-class. The new apartment had been vacated by a member of the congregation named Kenny Altman, a gay stand-up comedian who had decided to move to a larger space. Altman was the first *shul* member with whom Sarah made friends. He had formed a gay and lesbian *Havurah* or social group within the *shul* called *Keshet Havurah*, "Keshet" being the Hebrew word for

"rainbow." Altman's group had few precedents in conservative Judaism, and not everyone approved. Sarah made a
point of attending the *shabat* dinners that Altman and his
friends hosted in their homes and was one of the few non-
gay members of the *shul* to do so. After the initial resistance,
however, Altman was fully accepted by the community and
became the first openly gay person elected president of a
conservative congregation.

The building on Anza was the first among Sarah's residences to have an elevator. But although there was a larger
vacancy on the fourth floor, she chose Altman's apartment
on the first, puzzling Elissa, who asked her about it. Her
response was that she couldn't afford the larger one, but
when Elissa offered to pay the difference, she confessed the
real reason. If she took the fourth floor apartment she
would not be able to use the elevator on the Sabbath. Her
hip had so deteriorated by then, and there were days when
walking was so difficult, she was afraid she wouldn't be able
to climb the stairs when she came home.

But when the opportunity presented itself to climb
Masada, the legendary mountain fortress built by Herod
before the Christian era, she summoned all her reserves and
did. Masada was located in Israel and was the site of a
famous Jewish martyrdom. The Jews had seized it from the
Romans, who then laid siege to their settlement. The occu-
piers resisted the Roman armies until their defeat became
inevitable. Rather than live as slaves—their certain fate at
the hands of the Romans, they committed suicide *en masse*,
every man, woman, and child.

It was Rabbi Lew who offered the congregation the opportunity to climb Masada as part of a tour he was organizing to Israel. At the base of the mountain, a cable car to the top was available to visitors who did not want to endure the climb. But Sarah was determined to make the three-hour hike up the dirt "Snake Path" the Romans had built. The path derived its name from the jagged trajectory of its scale along the side of the thousand-foot cliff. "It was a winding and twisting path," remembers Christine Smith, who was on the trip. "It was miraculous that Sarah made it. She was really a trooper. We did a lot of walking and climbing over craggy things, but she always made it."

The dry heat eased the pain in Sarah's arthritic joint, making the climb a bit less difficult than she anticipated. Afterwards she commented, "My hip loves the desert." But her limp remained, and at one point when they were trekking through a ravine in the desert, her slow pace held up the others until the Israeli guide became so irritated he told Rabbi Lew she should be left behind in the bus. But Lew and the group stood by her and insisted she remain with them.

Sometimes her disabilities produced humorous moments. The first night in Israel her roommate said to her, "I have something to tell you." Sarah replied, "I have something to tell you too." "What is it?" the roommate asked. "I'm very hard of hearing," Sarah said, "so if you talk to me after the lights are out, I won't know what you said." Then it was Sarah's turn to ask, "What was it you were going to tell me?" At first her roommate tried to brush off the question.

"Never mind," she said. But Sarah insisted. "What were you going to tell me?" "Oh," the roommate said. "I was going to tell you I snore."

Sarah took two trips to Israel—in 2002 and 2003—and climbed Masada twice. She wrote brief journal notes about her visits:

Masada: We climbed Masada yesterday at the crack of dawn. The sun was a bright orange circle as it rose on top of the fortress. We visited Yad Vashem the day before, and the parallel between those who fought in the Warsaw Ghetto and the rebels on Masada who killed themselves rather than be killed and enslaved by the Romans was clear. These stories are sexier than the quieter ones of Jews studying the Torah in secret, quietly keeping Judaism alive. But if it had not been for them, a whole culture would have been lost.

Tel Aviv: On our way to dinner we passed Mike's Place, the recently bombed club, which looks completely restored. Tom Friedman says during the troubles in Beirut, you could measure the despair by whether or not people bothered to replace their bombed out windows. There is a resilience in the Israeli spirit that I admire.

Jerusalem: I am in an Internet café in a biblical city. I'm enjoying the juxtaposition of that. Israel is so much about different realities coexisting with each other, mystics and Mitnagdim, Moslems and Christians, old and new. We met with a Kabbalistic artist last night whose work was very much about juxtapositions too, the earthly and spiritual. He used to be part of the ultra-orthodox world but had difficulties there because of his interest in mysticism. He had the passion and openness you often find in people who have navigated seemingly opposed worlds. Earlier in Tel Aviv we heard the recording of the signing of Israel into a state. There were intense arguments about whether or not to include God in the declaration. The compromise was to refer to 'the rock of Israel.' To the religious it was a reference to one of the many names of God. To everyone else it was just a rock.

Her group went on a dig in ancient caves from the time of the Maccabees. "We found bones, shards of pottery, and an exquisite still intact oil lamp. Then we crawled through still unexcavated caves. The layers of history here are so thick, sometimes suffocating, sometimes rich with depth." They visited a community of orthodox Jews, the *Hareidi*, who ran a hospital operation serving people needing blood and bone marrow transplants:

We helped prepare food for hospital patients with *Hareidi* women and developmentally disabled adults. It was great to see this aspect of the *Hareidi* community, their commitment to living their practice. Watching them wearing their fur hats and black coats in the desert summer, it's easy to feel judgmental. There's a live tension between the rest of Israel and the *Hareidi* since the *Hareidi* don't serve in the army and receive a dispropor-

tionate amount of the welfare. I love it when my prejudices are challenged.

One of the events arranged for the trip was a talk given
by Rabbi Seth Mandell. "It was one of the saddest stories
I've heard," Sarah noted. While playing hooky from school,
Mandell's teenage son Koby wandered with a friend into a
cave where the two were accosted by Palestinian Arabs who
stoned them to death. Afterward Rabbi Mandell and his
wife created a camp for children who had been exposed to
terrorist attacks. They named the camp after their son.
Sarah was impressed by the rabbi's lack of bitterness but
wrote: "Seth will never be the same though."

When Sarah returned home, she brought back a menorah
from Jerusalem as a gift for me. It was made of cast iron and
painted gold, and would have weighed down an ordinary
shopping bag. I have no idea how many other gifts for family and friends she lugged on her return.

When she made a second visit to Israel, the country was
under siege from the second terrorist "Intifada." This was
the trip she made in secret, hiding from us her true destination, which she camouflaged as a spiritual retreat on Mount
Tamalpais. When she came back to America, she wrote a
story about her experience that juxtaposed the mundane
existence of the ordinary Israelis she had seen there with the
imminent violence that awaited them as Jews. The story
began, "I still shop in the *Machnei Yehudah* [the market-
place in Old Jerusalem] though Yossi would prefer I didn't,
since the bombing. I never shop there on Friday afternoon.

And I only shop in the Arab section for my kilo of coffee."
Sarah called her story, "Six Million Israelis Bought Milk."

By this time, she had become an avid student of Judaism,
which she described as "living inside a metaphor." She
explained the allusion saying that on the Sabbath

> you literally create stillness before the lights go on, and
> you have creation after the stillness. And on Pesach we
> live out the story of going from constriction to freedom.
> First, we do a compulsive cleaning, which puts us in a
> very narrow mind-set. Then we sit down to the Seder
> with our friends and family, and all this good food—and
> there's this sense of liberation. Of course, the Seder itself
> is a reenactment of the Exodus story: we're asked to tell
> the story as if we, ourselves, were brought out of Egypt.

One of the commentaries Sarah was asked to give at the
shul was on a portion from the Book of Numbers called
Parshah Chukat. This text inspired Sarah to reflect on the
religious dimension of all the stories that human beings create, including those she wrote herself. "At this point in our
story," she began, "the Israelites are at a critical and dark
juncture. Aaron dies. The Israelites mourn for thirty days.
Mirjam dies, and the water dries up. G-d has decreed that
this generation of Israelites will die in the desert. The generation that enters the Promised Land will have no memory of
slavery, but also no direct memory of revelation. What will
this generation bring into the Promised Land? And what do
we, many, many generations after Sinai carry with us?"

To answer the question she had posed, Sarah turned to a Chassidic tale about the great eighteenth century rabbi, the Baal Shem Tov. She proposed it as a way to understand the meaning of all stories.

When the Baal Shem Tov saw misfortune threatening the Jews, it was his custom to go into a certain part of the forest to meditate. There he would light a fire, say a special prayer, and a miracle would be accomplished and the misfortune averted. Later, when his disciple, the Maggid of Mezritch, had occasion to intercede with heaven for the same reason, he would go to the same place in the forest and say 'Master of the Universe, listen! I do not know how to light the fire, but I still can say the prayer.' And again, the miracle would be accomplished. Still later, Rabbi Moishe Leib of Sasov, in order to save his people once more, would go into the forest and say, 'I do not know how to light the fire, I do not know the prayer, but I know the place and this must be sufficient.' It was sufficient and the miracle was accomplished. Then it fell to Rabbi Israel of Rhizin to overcome misfortune. Sitting in his armchair, his head in his hands, he spoke to G-d. 'I am unable to light the fire and I do not know the prayer, and I cannot even find the place in the forest. All I can do is tell the story, and this must be sufficient.' And it was sufficient. For G-d made man, because G-d loves stories.

Sarah's commentary followed:

And so it is with us. We have the stories, and it is enough. First, there was the word. G-d spoke the world into existence. And we answer, each day with prayer. We speak our desires, fears, and regrets into existence. When we tell our stories from the heart, when we listen deeply, the separation between the listener and storyteller dissolves. We hear the truth of the *Shema* that we are one, there is one storyteller. And whenever that happens, G-d is present. It was Abraham's story of leaving his father's house, following G-d's call of *Lech Lecha* [go, leave] that was the beginning of the story, or stories, as we know them.

Sarah now turned to the fact that pre-biblical stories had no beginning, middle, and end.

Time was circular, an endless, repeating loop. Abraham's engaged and very personal relationship with G-d, his journey towards a new land, gave birth to a linear consciousness of time. The Israelites in Egypt did not have Abraham's experience of G-d, but they had his story. The story of Abraham's leave-taking allowed the Israelites to imagine their own journey from slavery to freedom. Suffering people all over the world have taken this story and absorbed it as their own. It is all our stories. It is the story of our heart, constricting and releasing, a story so powerful that each year we tell it again, as if we, ourselves had been brought out of Egypt.

Sarah put her stories and her talents at the service of people in need not only in Israel but around the world. In 2002, she became involved in the programs of the American Jewish World Service, an organization founded in 1985 and dedicated "to alleviating poverty, hunger and disease among the people of the developing world, regardless of race, religion or nationality." Its mission statement explains that the organization is "motivated by Judaism's imperative to pursue justice."

One of the commentaries Sarah gave in *shul* was on the obligation to strangers, in which she elaborated on the religious foundations of the American Jewish World Service.

"[G-d] upholds the cause of the fatherless and the widow, and befriends the stranger, providing him with food and clothing. You too must befriend the stranger, for you were strangers in the land of Egypt," we hear in this week's *Parshah Eikev*. The Torah reminds us of this because it is often too easy to turn away from the stranger. They are not kin; they are other. The rabbis of the Talmud also taught about the value of reaching outside our tribe. "We sustain the non-Jewish poor with the Jewish poor, visit the non-Jewish dead with the Jewish dead for the sake of peace."

Sarah went on to describe American Jewish World Service as "an organization that had befriended the stranger in Asia, Africa, and Latin America, partnering with them on entrenched and sometimes overwhelming challenges:

poverty, hunger, and illness." In 2002, Sarah signed up for a program that took her to El Salvador. The group of twenty was led by Beth Sholom's assistant rabbi, Dorothy Richman, and its mission was to help Salvadorans rebuild houses that had been destroyed in a hurricane.

Rabbi Richman recalls how excited Sarah was at the prospect of the trip and how she discussed the medical issues which might make some of the tasks too difficult for her. "But then she threw herself into it and worked in the fields with the rest of us." In El Salvador they met with Jose "Chencho" Alas. Alas was a former priest and leader of the liberation theology movement who had moved on from his radical commitments to develop a "theology of peace," and was by then a revered figure as a leader of El Salvador's rural poor.

"Sarah was very engaged by Chencho Alas," Rabbi Richman remembers. "He is an incredibly interesting and inspiring man. He met with our group and came to Beth Sholom several times. His view is that liberation theology is limited because it focuses on the poor against the rich. The theology of peace is for everyone." This was in perfect accord with Sarah's own feelings about social justice. "One of the things we would talk about as a group," explains Rabbi Richman, "is being in partnership with the Creator and having roles in the healing of the world. It's about an incremental healing. In some ways Sarah may have been radical but she was not impractical. She understood how the world worked."

After her return, Sarah wrote a report on what she had seen: "The Salvadorans were fast and efficient and didn't seem to require as many water breaks as we did. They were gracious though, and even joined us singing, and racing wheelbarrows. It was as if working together freed us temporarily from our roles as *campesinos* and privileged Americans. Work created a space beyond language where something deeper emerged, and we were no longer strangers." She then explained what the experience had meant to her: "In El Salvador I began to feel the way my spiritual life and my activism nurtured each other. I felt what Yeats expressed in his poem, 'Vacillation.'"

> *While on the shop and street I gazed*
> *My body of a sudden blazed;*
> *And twenty minutes more or less*
> *It seemed, so great my happiness,*
> *That I was blessed and could bless.*

During the trip, Rabbi Richman quipped to the group that one day she hoped to make a "Jews for Exegesis" t-shirt. Months after their return Sarah surprised her with a white polo shirt with those words artfully sewn on it. "You never knew what Sarah was picking up on," Rabbi Richman commented, "she always listened so intently to conversations, and then months, maybe years later, she'd remind you of a remark, an idea you had uttered and she had taken in."

The trip to Salvador was followed with another to Mumbai, India. This time she was accompanied by her mother and Ruth Messinger, the head of American Jewish World

Service. Their team met with organizations working to keep children out of the silk factories, to prevent domestic violence in the Muslim community, and to stop sex trafficking. It was on this trip that Sarah was taken violently ill, vomiting for days until dehydration threatened to drop her blood pressure to dangerous levels, causing Elissa to demand that a doctor come to her bedside.

Sarah's encounter with India's child labor industry reinforced her conviction that the practice was wrong, but, as usual, she had an awareness of the complexity of the problem. Seeing the actual levels of poverty in India, she wrote, "made me understand why Indians do not consider working for family to be 'child labor,'" but a matter of survival. What impressed her most on the trip was that she met Indian women who were changing their lives in a country encumbered with an ancient caste system. "It was extraordinarily inspirational to me, and I think forever changed my notion of what is possible," Sarah commented.

On one of the occasions when Sarah visited April and me in Malibu, she took a walk down the hill to the Pacific Coast Highway and was gone long enough to cause April to worry. Finally, April got into the car to look for her and found her wandering, anxious and lost, half a mile from the house. Sarah's reaction when April appeared was one of immediate relief. But once she was in the car she attempted to hide the fact that she had been lost, and acted as though nothing had happened. Whenever I think about Sarah's trips to exotic lands and places, I also think of the challenges she faced because of her poor sense of direction and near-sightedness and near deafness, which made the world a much bigger and more menacing prospect. But this never discouraged her quest to know and understand it.

Two years after the trip to El Salvador, she was off again, this time 10,000 miles away to the east coast of Africa on a mission to serve a tribe of African Jews in Uganda. She flew into Entebbe airport and then traveled by bus to the town of Mbele and then by cart to a little village with mud floor huts and no electricity or running water, where she would be staying with the tribe for the next two months.

The Abayudaya were Africans who had converted to Judaism during the First World War, as Sarah explained in a journal she kept:

> In a remote, rural part of eastern Africa, you can see men in brightly colored *kippot* and on *Shabbat* you can hear *Lecha Dodi* bursting out of the synagogue walls. The Abayudaya (the word means 'Jews' in their native Lugandan language) have been practicing Judaism since 1919. Their tribe leader, Semei Kukungulu, fed up with the British colonizers and missionaries went into seclusion and read the Bible for himself. He was moved by the God of Torah and disturbed that Christians had abandoned so many Biblical practices. He ripped out half of his Bible, keeping only the Five Books of Moses, and circumcised himself and his sons. Then he asked the tribe to follow Moses' commandments.
>
> In 1922, he built the first synagogue. For many years the Abayudaya were isolated from other Jews, but in

1936 they met a man named Joseph (from Yemen or Jerusalem, it's not clear which) who taught them about Rabbinic traditions such as Purim and Chanukah. Today they have five synagogues. They observe Shabbat and keep kosher. Some of their traditions are somewhat unique and based in Torah. At one of their synagogues, it is customary to take off your shoes, because God told Moses at the burning bush, 'Take off your shoes. This ground is holy.'

I spent two months living with the Abayudaya and teaching in the Hadassah Infant and Primary School. I taught nursery (3-5 year olds). It is a poor community and there are rarely enough books or pencils so students are working extra hard. The older children study in English which is a second language for them. While most of the families are poor farmers, the community is very rich in hospitality, community and family support, and music. The Abayudaya love to sing and dance, and their synagogue rocks every *Shabbat* with their own African-flavored tunes to the Jewish liturgy.

Sarah's trips abroad strengthened her love for her own country, which she saw as a place where people had gathered from all over the world to seek opportunity and justice. Some months before Sarah's death, Rabbi Micah Hyman, who had succeeded Rabbi Lew at Beth Sholom, challenged the congregation to come up with a prayer for the country to be included in the regular service. The congregation adopted Sarah's submission:

Prayer For the Country
Ribono Shel Olam,

Let America Be America
Let it be my Land
Let it be your Land
From the curvaceous hills of California
to the New York Islands
Let our tired, our poor, our huddled masses
finally breathe free
Let our leaders pursue justice, justice, justice
Let them be mindful that we are all created
*   equal, b'tzelem elohim,*
Protect our leaders from the seductions of power
Protect our right to protest, to insist we can do
*   better*
Protect us all from those who would do us harm
Let America be America
And let us say, Amen

The weekend before her funeral there was a family gathering at the Los Altos home of Ben and Felicia. Elissa drove down with Sarah, and Felicia's parents came up from Los Angeles, arriving on Friday to attend a charity ball to benefit a camp for autistic children that Mariah attended. Ben and Felicia were benefactors of the camp. On Sunday everyone clustered around the island in Felicia's kitchen where the food and desserts were laid out. Sarah was barely taller than the counter. On such occasions she would stand on the outer rim of the circle of hungry adults and patiently weave her way in toward the food when a space opened up. She had learned to find her passages through life like that.

Everyone remembered a comment that Felicia's father made to Sarah in the course of the afternoon that gave her special pleasure. John Wiley's grandparents had been slaves in Louisiana and his family were sharecroppers. He went to work on oil pipelines, following them west from Shreveport to California after the Second World War. A lifetime of hard work had enabled him to buy a house in Carson, a middle-class suburb south of Los Angeles. His daughter, Felicia, who was the first member of her family to go to college, had graduated from the University of Southern California. After they were married, Felicia and Ben moved into the house I had bought in Griffith Park, where they stayed with their infant daughter Julia until Ben finished his masters at UCLA. Now Julia was a young woman of nineteen, completing her freshman year at Columbia University. She was planning a summer trip to Argentina to work on a project to help the poor. Remarking on his granddaughter's plans, John Wiley said to Sarah: "Julia is walking in your footsteps." It was just the right recognition of Sarah's often unnoticed impact, and it caused her to break into a very broad smile.

Sarah's impact was a topic of conversation for the whole family in the year that followed. When Barack Obama was elected the first black president of the United States, everyone remembered Sarah's Iowa campaign. Anne, who was not political and had vowed not to watch the election returns, could not keep her resolve. When the vote put Obama over the top she called Elissa and said to her: "Sarah won."

We buried her in the brightly colored *kippah* she had been given by the Abayudaya. After the funeral, we received a letter from Sebagabo Moses, an elder of the tribe: "I am very saddened to hear of our beloved friend passing. I personally remember her as a beautiful, strong soul and very smiling lady with a good nature and generous spirit of Judaism. Now she goes to her rest in peace, to be gathered, in among her ancestors and her people. I send my blessings to her family and all of the House of Israel to be comforted among the Mourners of Zion. May her memory be a blessing. Amen."

To encourage others to follow in her footsteps, Ben endowed a scholarship fund in Sarah's name at American Jewish World Service. Anne wrote the mission statement which concluded: "This fund has been set up so that others may continue her quest to bring education, spirituality, love, and strength—the Gifts of Sarah—to those in need, to continue to bring the spirit of Sarah Rose to the far corners of the world and to keep that spirit alive within ourselves."

During the "*shloshim*" service which follows a funeral by thirty days, Elissa was struck by how many people in attendance mentioned Sarah's disabilities and praised the way she overcame them. Sitting among these mourners, Elissa thought how Sarah would have been mortified, if she were alive, to hear herself talked about as "disabled." The thing Sarah hated most about herself, she thought, was her disabilities. At that moment, she remembered what Rabbi Lew had written in his autobiography about "divine names."

Rabbi Lew's discussion of the subject took as its text the story of Jacob, who wrestled with God and received a new name—a divine name—"Israel," which means "struggled with God." His former name, "Jacob," is derived from the root, *ekev*, which means "heel." It was said that coming out of the womb Jacob grabbed onto his brother Esau's heel in an attempt to be the first born. Eventually Jacob cheated Esau out of his birthright and later sought to marry the youngest daughter of Laban rather than wooing the oldest who by tradition should have been married first. Thus, Jacob was the *supplanter*—never satisfied with who he was, always seeking another's place.

Following his summary of these biographical facts, Rabbi Lew commented on Jacob's transformation into Israel: "Here in this encounter with his own dark side, Jacob learns that the very thing he couldn't understand about himself, his refusal to accept the way things are, is his divine name—*Israel*: 'He struggled with God.' This is perhaps the most profound psychological transformation it is possible to undergo: the realization that the very thing we can't stand about ourselves is our divine name, our uniqueness, the way God has made us, the quality that gives our life its shape and meaning." And so it was with my daughter, Sarah.

When this manuscript was complete, I sent it to Rabbi Lew and he wrote back:

Sarah was, in all likelihood, my only true disciple. Every time you cite a teaching of Sarah's on a biblical passage or on a meditation or on a social justice issue, I recognize my own teaching in it, but also how Sarah had assimilated that teaching and transformed it and made it wholly new and completely her own. I am pretty sure that no one else has ever honored me in this way, and although I enjoyed these parts of the book immensely, they also helped me to understand why I've taken her loss so hard. A great student is a once in a lifetime thing, and Sarah was mine.

8

A Cracking of the Heart

It is a fact of our communal lives that we understand each other only through ourselves, and therefore not well. Writing a memoir about my daughter disclosed things about her that led me to reflect ruefully on the ways I had failed to appreciate her, or respond to her adequately, or support her sufficiently while she was alive. There is nothing left for me to do with these regrets now but to embrace them.

Since we cannot enter another's consciousness, we are forced to rely on our own stories for reference points through which our encounters make sense. This is a fateful narcissism that colors our vision and creates our conflicts. Yet the same self-regard also provides a bridge that allows us to heal them. This is the meaning of Sarah's *tikkun olam*: while we are many, we are one.

Because Sarah and I were writers, we found it natural to converse through our work. Since mine was public, it afforded her opportunities to ask me about the events that had led to our divergent paths. In this way, the facts that separated us became points of contact. She was curious about my history, and I was eager to hear her opinions and answer her questions. Pursuing these ends, we were able to open lines of communication that our tangled family narratives had previously blocked.

Long before Sarah embarked on her world mission, the murder in Oakland had set me on a course that put us at odds. Until that moment my politics had been a pursuit of social justice that was closer to a religious calling than a search for practical solutions. The crusades I joined did not seek adjustments to the framework of ordinary human disappointments. Their goals were more grandiose: to transform the framework itself. But the murder of an innocent woman by members of my progressive faith persuaded me that the world would not be saved by the very creatures who had made it what it was.

While Sarah was setting up her household on Bush Street, I was completing my memoir, *Radical Son*. Before submitting the manuscript to the publisher, I sent her a copy. When her comments came back, they were not so much concerned with the conclusions I had reached as with the way I approached my subjects. She wanted me to be less dismissive of political opponents and more appreciative of their human complexity. Although I no longer remember the specifics of these complaints, I readily accepted her advice.

These concerns re-surfaced a decade later when she sent me a detailed critique of an article I had written about

Bettina Aptheker, a political activist whose father had been a leader of the Communist Party. My article was a review of the autobiography that Aptheker had recently published. I was interested in her as someone who had not had second thoughts, as I had, about the radical commitments that had absorbed her life. In my review, I drew a harsh picture of the household she grew up in, describing it as one that "routinely required the suppression of facts inconvenient to [the] cause," and characterizing her as someone who doggedly followed her father's rigid example, impervious to views that challenged her own.

Sarah commented:

This is a nice synopsis, but the reader is going to want more insight from you as someone who has struggled with an ideology handed down by parents. To paraphrase you, 'Where's the life?...' Where's the empathy for how difficult it can be to sever yourself from a powerful ideology? What we get instead is a kind of checklist: She compared her family dynamics to a Stalinist gulag: good. She stayed with the Communist Party: bad. You're basically telling us that you went into this book with a closed mind & a chip on your shoulder. This sets you up as someone with an axe to grind & sets a tone of condescending contempt (never mind, we women are used to that).

I emailed her back: "Well, this is harshly put, but I get your point, and it's a good one. I will definitely look to develop a more empathetic commentary when I return to the text." And so it went through the length of the article I had written. It was always a pleasure to engage in these dialogues with my daughter, and I always felt the better for them.

After the publication of *Radical Son*, I continued to question the beliefs that had brought tragedy to my own life and even greater sorrows for others. The book that followed was called *The Politics of Bad Faith* and was prefaced with an epigraph from the great heretic of Soviet Communism, Alexander Solzhenitsyn. The epigraph encapsulated the truth Solzhenitsyn had won through a radical life and through immense suffering: "Gradually, it was disclosed to me that the line separating good and evil passes not through states, nor between classes, nor between political parties either—but right through the human heart, and through all human hearts." It was the conclusion I had come to through my own experience.

While Sarah was alive, I failed to appreciate the extent to which she shared this insight. Nor did I fully comprehend the ways in which it had shaped her choices. Although she was involved in progressive causes, her commitments were never consuming like mine. The passions that governed her interests were literary and moral, and they served as a check on what she believed humanly possible. Nonetheless, she was drawn to the social causes of the Left both by friends and by her own inclinations.

In the spring of 1985, when Sarah was twenty-one, and just before she moved into the Haight Street apartment,

Peter Collier and I wrote an article that caused a stir when it appeared in the *Washington Post*. The two of us had been leaders of the New Left during the 1960s but revealed in the article that we had recently voted for its nemesis, Ronald Reagan. In a calculated gesture we couched our disclosure in abrasive New Left style: "Casting our ballots for Ronald Reagan was indeed a way of finally saying goodbye to all that—to the self-aggrandizing romance with corrupt Third Worldism; to the casual indulgence of Soviet totalitarianism; to the hypocritical and self-dramatizing anti-Americanism which is the New Left's bequest to mainstream politics."

These were not words designed to ingratiate us with the San Francisco communities in which Sarah had found a cultural home. "Can you believe it," she said to her sister Anne, half joking. "Dad's gone over to the dark side." And then: "Oh well, that's dad."

My political turn was a topic of discussion among all my children. "Everybody in Berkeley was saying you had sold out and things like that," Ben remembers. "Anne and Jon and I gave you the benefit of the doubt, but Sarah was pretty diligent and thoughtful about it. She read all you wrote, and thought about the reasons you gave carefully. This was true of the way she approached all political issues. I would have conversations with her about the minimum wage and sweat shops in the underdeveloped world, generally defending the market system. But even though her sympathies were with the left, she never had an instant reaction or judgment. She was interested in the details behind the headlines, and always weighed what she heard."

One impetus behind Sarah's activism was Emily. After leaving San Francisco State, she had moved to Los Angeles to work for an anti-nuclear group called the Alliance for Survival and also the *Catholic Worker*, whose members were active in feeding the homeless. When she returned to the Bay Area, she brought her political contacts and interests with her. Sarah accompanied her on demonstrations and was swept up in their enthusiasms. But she always remained more interested in individuals than crowds, devoting most of her political energies to the appeals she wrote in behalf of political prisoners. Her identification with the Left and its causes raised my anxieties about where she might be heading and became a source of occasional frictions between us.

I am haunted now by the memory of one of these conflicts though it occurred more than twenty years ago. It was an event so painful to me, even in memory, that it changed forever the way I approached my daughter over political matters. It also marked a turning away in my personal relationships from the combative disposition that had been a second nature to me, and that Rabbi Lew would undoubtedly regard as my "divine name."

I had come up to the East Bay from Los Angeles and taken the family to dinner at a local restaurant, seating myself opposite my children with Sarah diagonally to my right. My move to Los Angeles had put an added distance between us, and was still fresh, as was the commotion created by my political turn. The conversation soon drifted away from the personal to more distant political themes. The subject I selected for discourse was the danger of "anti-war" movements whose purpose, I believed, was to disarm democracies and encourage their enemies. I did not connect this indictment to any specific parties or to the activities of any of my children, but Sarah was a participant in peace causes, as we all understood.

Even if Sarah had not been so involved I should been more careful about venting opinions on so charged a subject. In this period of my life I was unable to speak about such matters without passions rising unbidden that were near ferocious. It was an animus fed by the still-fresh pain from Betty's murder and the indignation I had cultivated all my life as an advocate for social causes. An additional factor was my fear—present since the divorce—of losing authority with my children and, worse, their affection. I did not want my children to become prey to the same illusions that had once ensnared me. But these were hardly excuses for the emotion that spilled into the dinner conversation as I went on heedlessly with my attack.

The assault continued until the moment I became aware of the expression on my daughter's face. Sarah had been silent throughout my tirade, which I hardly noticed as I barreled ahead. But all of a sudden her features came into my view with an excruciating clarity. I saw that her eyes had grown red and liquid, and her face was convulsed as though an immense weight was pressing inexorably down on her. Her expression in that instant was one of such mute and irremediable suffering that the distress of it has never left me.

Seeing my daughter's unhappiness, knowing that I was its cause, brought me up short. I stopped my harangue and paused to collect myself. Then, in a voice hoarse with shame, I attempted to turn the conversation away from its contentious themes, and fell into silence. Even then I knew I should have done more—should have attempted to undo directly what I had done. But I was unable to do so. Trapped in an emotional paralysis, which was born of the recriminations and griefs that had become a dominant feature of myself, I was unable to retreat from the words I had uttered without feelings of self-betrayal. But at the same time I could not block the terrible sight of my daughter in pain, or the realization that I was its author. As the conversation shifted to other voices, I hid in my silence and thought: "Who is this angry person? What sort of individual could do this to his child?"

For the next twenty years, while I was still privileged to have her in my life, I carried the shame and anguish of that moment with me. Whenever I recollected it, I felt the same helpless misery and guilt, and worked as best I could to make it up to her. From that day to her last, whatever conflicts we had, I never again allowed myself to indulge such bitterness or be so blind to her feelings and beliefs. I never did another thing to reduce her to tears or to inflict such pain. Yet I can never forget that I did.

The Day of Atonement in the Jewish calendar comes during a sequence of observances whose significance is reflected in the word *Teshuvah*, which means both "turning" and "repentance." Rabbi Lew wrote a book-length meditation about these rituals, which he called *This Is Real And You Are Completely Unprepared.* He meant by this that none of us are prepared for life and its impending end. Of the spiritual turning which takes place during the Days of Awe, Lew wrote: "This is a journey from denial to awareness, from self-deception to judgment. We will earn our Divine Name. We will move from self-hatred to self-forgiveness, from anger to healing, from hard-heartedness to broken-heartedness." He employed the metaphor "a cracking of the heart," to describe how this process begins.

While Sarah was alive, I was careful not to pry into the lives of those she depended on. I knew Rabbi Lew's importance to her but did not point our discussions in his direction or seek to identify his particular influence on her thoughts. I wanted to prevent my agendas from interfering with ours, as they had in the past. I did not want my knowledge of the directions my daughter had taken to come from anyone but herself. It was a well-advised caution. When I mentioned that Sarah was a member of Beth Sholom to an orthodox friend, he responded: "Oh, that hippie rabbi from Berkeley. My condolences." But I kept my own counsel and withheld judgment and never let such prejudices color my views or reflect on hers.

It was not until after Sarah was gone that I obtained a copy of *One God Clapping*, the autobiography Rabbi Lew had written. Reading it, I discovered affinities between us I would never have suspected. As I went over the chapters of his life, I saw that we were, in a manner of speaking, spiritual kin. When I mentioned this to Elissa, she said "I always thought Sarah was taken with Rabbi Lew because he was like you."

Lew and I disagreed in many of our political choices, but we shared a fundamental understanding of the ambitions behind them. Living in Berkeley he had encountered many activists for whom politics was not a matter of seeking practical compromises for problems that ultimately had no solution. For them, politics was the quest for a redemption in this world and it inflamed them with the self-righteous feelings that accompanied such hopes. Among the radicals he encountered were members of the Symbionese Liberation Army who had kidnapped Patty Hearst, and also the right-wing followers of Reverend Moon who had joined a totalitarian cult. In Lew's account of the illusions that inspired these political missionaries, he invoked the Buddhist insight that "all suffering is caused by *tana*, the selfish desire for something other than what is. . . ."

The desire for a world that is fundamentally different from the one we have been given was the precise hubris I had found troubling in the radical cause. As Lew had written, revolutionaries and redeemers "put a romantic overlay over life. . . they [played] on the most ancient of all human impulses, the desire to cover over the yawning emptiness of our real experience with something else . . . a fairy tale, a savior." In *The End of Time*, I had expressed a similar thought: "The evil of this world is not caused by ignorance of the good, or failure to appreciate the holiness of human life. It is caused by the black hole that lies at the bottom of every human soul." It was out of the desire to fill this hole that radical dreams were born.

One of the papers Sarah left behind in her apartment was a page from the manuscript of *The End of Time* I had sent her that contained a criticism of these radical hopes. In making my criticism, I had inadvertently challenged the idea that connected her spiritual and political worlds. This was the Jewish concept of a *tikkun olam*—the idea of a "repair of the world." In the Kabbalistic tradition, which was its source, *tikkun olam* involved a returning of the entire world to God through human actions. It was the idea of an earthly redemption, which was the heart of the radical project, and was why I inveighed against it. But this was not, as I was eventually to realize, Sarah's idea.

As I look back on our conversations, I recall now that Sarah directed me to a rabbinic tradition that warns against a "hurrying of the messiah"—the presumption that human beings can achieve divine ends. Jewish history contains many famous examples of false prophets like Shabbatai Zvi who promised his followers the end of days and brought them catastrophe instead. The rabbis' warnings that Sarah referred to mirrored my own. Perhaps I didn't listen carefully enough to her at the time; perhaps I was so absorbed by what *I* wanted to tell *her* that I didn't fully take in what she was saying to me. Whatever the cause, I failed to appreciate the fact that this rabbinic idea was *her* tradition and *her* meaning. Instead I responded to her comments as though we were merely discussing an idea, unrelated to who and what she was.

Consequently, when I inveighed against radical illusions in my book, I did so in terms that were uncompromising and without nuance, and that struck at my daughter's faith:

"What I had learned through the most painful experiences of my life," I wrote, "was to pay attention to the differences. It was a lesson at odds with the moral teachings that have come down to us across the millennia. All the prophets—Moses, Jesus, Buddha, the Hindu gurus—have taught the opposite truth: that however different we may look and act, we are one. High and low, strong and weak, virtuous and sinful, we are all incarnations of the same divine spirit. Underneath our various skins, all are kin." Then I asked: "Do we really regard ourselves as one with rapists and murderers? Or should we? Many try to believe it, but I cannot embrace this radical faith. I feel no kinship with those who can cut short a human life without remorse; or with terrorists who target the innocent; or with adults who torment small children for the sexual thrill. I suspect no decent soul does either."

In writing these words, I failed to take into account what she had said about these issues, or to appreciate their depths. It was a milder version of what had occurred twenty years before but this time she was able to defend herself, and did. On the back of the page I had sent were these hand-written comments:

First, have a little humility. You are not smarter than Moses, Jesus and Buddha. Note that you praise Jesus' peacefulness when it's politically convenient—slamming Islam.

She was referring to the way I had contrasted Jesus, the man of peace, with Mohammed, the conqueror, who had declared war on unbelievers.

But you have no respect for how Jesus got there. This is a serious practice for me, one I take on every single day. It's about seeing people in the fullness of their humanity. They are not *just* child molesters, rapists, adulterers. And how pathetically easy to pat yourself on the back for not being a child molester. If you have no desire for something in the first place, resisting it is no problem.

She went on:

Back to the practice: If you see someone in the fullness of their humanity, you see how they are acting out their own confusion and suffering. This does *not* justify hurtful or evil acts. It doesn't even always inspire forgiveness. *But* if you see someone this way, you respond more in sadness than in anger. And that is simply a more excellent state of being. Even if you've never had this experience (and more's the pity), *respect* the experience of those who have. I'm not talking about an idea either. This is a full-bodied understanding of another person. This practice has in fact transformed all my relationships, *including ours by the way.*

For some reason, she never sent me these comments, or if she did, I failed again to understand them.

I wish now that I had.

I wish I could tell her that I agree with her that we achieve a more excellent state of being when we see ourselves in others.

I wish I could tell her that I agree with her about the humanity of criminals, which is the complement to Solzhenitsyn's warning that evil runs through the human heart, and through all human hearts.

I wish I could tell her how much I regret the fact that anger from my wounds, which I vented through my weakness, was undoubtedly the cause of many of her silences, and of anguish about which I can only guess. And how sorry I am for that.

I wish I could tell her how moved I am by the example she set and by what she was able to accomplish in the brief time given to her.

I wish I could thank her for the affirmations of her father that I found in the writings she left behind.

I wish I could tell her how much I miss her.

Among the affirmations she left were comments contained in an email correspondence we exchanged just before she died. They were inspired by an "open letter" I had written to my friend Christopher Hitchens in response to a book he had published called *God Is Not Great: How Religion Poisons Everything.*

"Dear Christopher...Is it the case that religion poisons everything or is it we who poison everything, including religion?"

Sarah's comment in capital letters was: "YES!"

In my letter, I argued that if religions were man-made as Christopher claimed, and if the fear of death made the desire for a meaningful life inescapable, as he seemed to concede, there was no way for human beings to be anything but religious, even when they were anti-religious. Thus atheism was itself a religious faith, and his campaign against God was merely helping to construct a spiritual vacuum which would inevitably be filled by other gods and equally zealous secular creeds. In our lifetimes, I reminded him, these secular passions—Communism in particular—had produced "even more terrible results than [the religions] they replaced."

Sarah's comment, again in capital letters, was: "YES."

Then she added: "His lumping socialism and religion together is very convenient and not intellectually honest." She was referring to Christopher's cavalier dismissal of the crimes committed by Communists and other totalitarian atheists. Christopher had managed to evade this problem by calling Communism a "religion," which in the broad sense was true but made his argument circular.

I took great pleasure in these exchanges with my daughter, which by then had become almost routine. Three years earlier, when we completed our back and forth over my review of Bettina Aptheker's book, I sent her a note:

> I really appreciate all the effort you put into this. I greatly enjoy our exchanges, and am grateful for your insights, even when we disagree. Last year, Sherman Alexie sent me an email on New Year's thanking me for being his friend because it was important to have friends (and family) whom you disagree with. It enlarged your humanity and taught you empathy and compassion. I feel that way about our correspondence and interactions. I feel better

as a person as a result of our engagements. I hope you do too.

> I love you,
> Dad

My daughter replied:

I totally agree with Sherman Alexie. I read a book where the main character has this debate about Israel with her cousin and says, "You're not a Zionist. If you were, we couldn't be friends." And I was horrified, not just for the rejection of someone for his ideas, but for all that's lost when you close your mind that way.

> I love you, too.
> Sarah

○   ○   ○

Before coming to see her that final evening I made a reservation at Green's Restaurant, which was located by the water in the San Francisco Marina. When I suggested the location, she posted back "Green's is great," as I knew she would. Built in a converted warehouse in the Fort Mason complex, the restaurant featured a famous vegetarian menu. It was a creation of the San Francisco Zen Center, where Rabbi Lew received his training in Buddhism. If I had known this would be our last supper, I couldn't have chosen a more fitting place to have it.

A light rain was falling, and it was already dark when I left my downtown hotel to make the drive to her apartment.

Starting out, I had to navigate my way through a nightmare tangle of evening traffic caused by a parade to celebrate the Chinese New Year. Despite the weather, a crowd of pedestrians in plastic raincoats and umbrellas was blocking the streets. Taking a circuitous route from downtown, I reached Geary and began the drive west towards the Richmond District. Once I was free of the downtown streets, the traffic eased up, and I soon arrived on the little slope of Anza where I parked in the driveway and climbed the two flights of stairs to her apartment and knocked.

When the door opened, I sensed immediately that something was wrong. Her forehead was knotted and her expression one of marked discomfort. But despite what happened later at dinner, I do not think, in retrospect, that this reflected any displeasure with me. It seemed more like the distress that would accompany a physical disorder such as cramps or an acid stomach. Until the moment of letdown, I hadn't realized how much I looked forward to the smile that always greeted me when she appeared in the doorway, as though my visit was an unexpected gift. I didn't inquire into the source of her distress in part because whatever was bothering her did not seem that severe, and in part because of her normal injunction against inquiries into her health. On the other hand, if she had an issue with me, I knew it would surface during dinner.

On our ride to the Marina, it was I who carried the small talk, which included some self-deprecating observations about my driving and the fact that I had momentarily lost my way before happily finding it again. When we finally arrived in the Fort Mason parking lot, I stopped the car and the two of us stepped out into the weather to begin our trudge through the darkness at an achingly slow pace. A wind from the Bay swept the rain into our faces, intensifying the chill. As we side-stepped the puddles I noticed that her limp had become more pronounced and found myself worrying again about her health.

We finally reached the entrance and pushed through the doors carved from massive planks of black walnut, then entered the warm interior. Green's is famously fitted in twelve varieties of woods, and is backed by a wall of latticed windows looking out on the boats in the yacht basin. It was a Saturday evening and, though early, the place was already filling up. In the lounge area, people were sipping drinks and waiting for their tables, some standing, others seated on stumps cut from maple and cherry trees that had been varnished to look like *objets d'art*.

Fortunately, we had timed our reservation well, so that while we were looking over the crowd the hostess came up and summoned us to follow her. Not long after we were seated a waitress appeared to take our orders. The menu at Green's is a four-course dinner with a set price, but Sarah passed on her appetizer. Perhaps she was on a diet. After making my choices, I ordered a second appetizer "for the table" in case Sarah relented and looked over in her direction to see if she objected. When the orders came she nibbled at the edges from the one she liked. This pleased me, not only because she seemed to be enjoying the food, but because I knew then I had made the right decision.

As the meal progressed, we chatted about the elections and other subjects more mundane. I asked her about the *shul* and the problems I knew were facing the congregation. Rabbi Lew had retired, and there had been difficulties finding a suitable replacement. One rabbi had come and gone; another had been hired. I asked how he was doing. The *shul* had just completed an expensive building project and was putting new programs in place, and Sarah had plenty to say about both. Soon we were enjoying the conversational flow, and it was time I thought to bring up an issue that had been concerning me for days, which her distressed look at the door had done nothing to put to rest.

It was about our email correspondence, whose volume had picked up after her trip to Iowa. We had been trading observations and clippings about the election and other matters, often several times a day. In the course of our exchanges, we had become locked in a dispute about conservative Christians and their support for Israel, which she found suspect. Although I tried several arguments, I couldn't induce her to warm up to the idea that they might genuinely support Israel without ulterior agendas. And then her emails stopped.

So I brought up the subject. "I haven't been getting any emails from you. Are you upset with me?" The answer came back like a missile: "What happened to all that liberal compassion?" she said. These were the precise words I had used in the email I had sent before she went silent. It was my effort at humor designed to tease her into reconsidering her position. Although the remark was offered in a light-hearted spirit, I didn't make the mistake now of brushing off her sharp reaction. She had taken it as a slight. I apologized. I was wrong to have said it and was sorry to have upset her. I missed her emails.

As she listened to the apology, a glimmer of satisfaction flitted across her face, which she tried to suppress. Then she nodded by way of acknowledgment. But I knew this concession didn't necessarily mean I was going to get the pleasure of her correspondence back anytime soon. I hadn't forgotten the "write faster" episode, and bated my breath. It was a welcome relief, when I returned to Los Angeles, to find the emails had resumed.

The waitress came to take our dessert orders, and again Sarah passed. Again, I put in a second order "for the table." When they were served, Sarah reached out and picked daintily at the pumpkin gelato and then at the carob pastry. When we had finished, we went back out into the cold rain and the darkness, and made the long trek to the car. I drove through the glistening streets to her apartment and stopped the car in the driveway next to her front steps. I leaned over to kiss her goodnight and said I hoped she would be coming down to Los Angeles soon to see us. Now that she had completed her teaching credential and her night school was over, she would have more time. She said she would. April and I always looked forward to her visits, because they were especially good times for the three of us. I liked being able to talk to her at leisure, when I could learn more about her life than phone conversations or email correspondence allowed. In recent years, these times together had been a warm pleasure for us both, and this time there would be an added bonus. April and I had moved into a new house in a rural valley and had acquired two horses. Sarah was fond of our other animals, and we were eager to show her the new additions.

The next day Elissa picked her up at the Anza apartment. Together they drove down the peninsula to Los Altos for the family gathering at Ben and Felicia's. And that was the last time any of us saw Sarah alive.

o   o   o

Death is brutal and is no respecter of persons. There are no reprieves from its judgment and there is no justice in its works. After years of struggle, Sarah's life was finally on the verge of becoming easier. She had worked for more than a decade to get a Masters Degree that would qualify her for a regular teaching position. For all those years, she had taken multiple buses every night to get to school and back, while working a day job to support herself. Now the bus rides were behind her, and her economic circumstances were improving as well. Her maternal grandmother and her aunt Barbara had both left her a little money. My son Ben had created a successful business and given her some stock from the company he built. With this security, she was already planning new travels to serve people in need around the world. And with her new free time, she could finish the book we were going to put together of her writings.

I do not really know why we all forgot about the prediction of an early death for Turner Syndrome children. Perhaps it was because Sarah always had so much life in her, right to the end.

When death takes someone you love, you are left with a hole in your heart that will never be filled, and a well of pain that will never be emptied. "How *are* you?" Elissa asked me three months after she was gone. "How are we supposed to live through this?"

I can take a small satisfaction in the fact that death's victory over my daughter remains incomplete. For though she is gone, she has left me this gift: When I see a homeless person destitute on the street, I think of Sarah, and my heart opens. If there is a criminal shut behind bars, I force myself to remember her compassion, and a sadness shades my anger. If there is a child languishing in need, I think of my daughter in a mud floor hut ministering to the children of the Abayudaya tribe, and my heart goes out to them. These images and their influence are an incarnation of her life after life, her rolling of the soul, her *gilgul hanefesh*. Whenever I think of Sarah, tears well in my eyes, and my chest fills to the brim; and then I am overwhelmed by the terrible sorrow of our human lot and how finally, in this, we are one.

o   o   o

The cemetery where she was laid to her final rest is reserved for members of Beth Sholom and, like the *shul* itself, is called Home of Peace. Despite the name, our visit to the grave site proved to be one of the most trying passages in our goodbyes. There was something so terminal about putting our daughter in the ground. When Elissa and I went to choose her plot and I looked out at the grassy incline where the graves were laid out, I had a dark fantasy of her struggling to breathe under the earth, and was forced to look away.

We picked a spot under a shade tree on the gentle rise of the cemetery hillside. When the mourners assembled for the burial, the sun was shining and the greenery was so lush it seemed a rebuke to our purpose. Folding chairs had been placed around the freshly dug grave and a mound of black earth was piled next to the pit. Sarah's friend Joel was there, and so were Elizabeth and Mirjam, and Kenny Altman, and Henry and Katherine Hollander, and Rabbi Lew. Rabbi Hyman stepped forward to lead the *kaddish* for the dead and Emily sang the 23rd Psalm. *The Lord is my shepherd.* Then the rabbi handed me a shovel with its back turned up, a Jewish custom to symbolize the opposition of death to life, and I cast in the first clod.

I had been to other burials and knew how jarring it could be for those who had to shovel earth on the coffin, to close the lid on the ones they loved and reconcile themselves to the fact that they were not coming back. My son Jon was the only one of my surviving children to step forward and pitch the sod in. Later, my daughter Anne said that the entire ritual of putting her sister in the ground was too much. "It just seemed so final, so permanent. I was worried I might jump in to give her one last hug."

This was exactly what I was thinking when her mother fell suddenly to her knees from the chair on which she was grieving and crawled to the top of the dirt pile. There was an audible gasp from the mourners as she clutched the earth and threw it over the edge onto her daughter's coffin, as though she wanted to follow it in.

She had nursed this child in infancy and bathed its troubled limbs; she had spent anxious hours waiting outside hospital operating rooms, and had looked on with pride at her daughter's graduations and other rites of passage; she had sat in her audiences at public readings, and accompanied her to Turner Society meetings in cities near and far, and had marched alongside her on demonstrations; she had crossed the oceans to join her in the slums of India, and had wept when Sarah read the prayer for the dead at her sister Barbara's funeral; together they had prepared family *seders*, and had dined with each other more than with any other person in their lives; just two months before, she had been there in the airport at three in the morning to greet Sarah on her return from Iowa with the triumphant news that her cause had won. Through all the years, Elissa had been Sarah's principal confidante and support, and Sarah hers, and now she could not imagine a life without her.

Bone thin and washed in tears, wraith-like and paler than pale in her mourning black, Elissa clutched at our daughter's earthly shroud, and I reflected how life for us had become a downward slope, and how rising had now become its most daunting task. And then I thought of what Sarah had left behind to inspire us to do just that.

o   o   o

Three months after we buried her, spring turned to summer, and the skeletal garden in front of the Berkeley house came back with a flourish, exfoliating in petal reds and leafy greens. On a bright morning, moving among the bougainvillea and vines, Elissa came upon the stalk of a single white rose. "I never believed in the idea of a spiritual presence before," she said when she told me of her find. "But no one planted a white rose in that garden, and none ever appeared before now. I can't look at it, without thinking of Sarah."

Like her mother, I am skeptical about mystical phenomena. But, like her, I believe in my daughter, and in her exemplary life, and I feel her presence every day.

9

More Important
Than Sadness

When I came to the end of this book, I went up to San Francisco to finally meet Rabbi Lew. I had invited him to dinner and for the occasion he had selected the Millenium restaurant, which was Sarah's other favorite vegetarian dining place. It was located in the lobby of the Hotel California on Geary, a short distance from where I was staying, and I was the first to arrive. When the rabbi and his wife appeared, his cheeks had a slight flush replacing the ashen pallor I remembered from the memorial service. On that occasion, we had not spoken except to greet each other, a fact that puzzled me at the time. But my efforts since then to solicit his comments on the manuscript I had written and to make arrangements for our dinner caused me to realize that even though his calling thrust him into the lives of strangers, he was in his heart a shy and introspective person. As we seated ourselves at the table, I was overwhelmed with feelings of affection for this sweet man who had taken such good care of my daughter and been such a profound influence in her life.

Weeks earlier, when I contacted him to set up the evening, he had not been feeling well. I asked him about his health and about the pressures of his work, lecturing and teaching since his retirement from the synagogue. He said that travel was becoming harder for him, and this prompted us to share notes on our schedules and to commiserate with each other on how getting older made them more difficult. We talked about Sarah and their trips to Israel, and he and his wife recalled how hardy she had been on the climb to Masada and how the guide had tried to persuade them to leave her on the bus because she was so slow. He then repeated what he had written to me when I sent him the manuscript to read—that Sarah was his one true disciple.

As the evening wore on, we talked about the points where our own lives had intersected, the college we had both attended and the cities we had both lived in, though our paths had never crossed. I inquired about his plan to write a history of his family through four generations, a project he had mentioned in his memoir. He was going to call it *The Life That Ran Through Me*. He said the book was already completed and he was looking for a publisher, and I offered to help him find one. I noted that my seventieth birthday was coming up in two weeks and we talked about what we would do with the next ten years if we were given them.

I felt a powerful desire to be friends with this man, and to have been friends with him for all those years when we had not known each other but had pursued life journeys that seemed so different but were not. When I returned home after the dinner, I waited for him to contact me about helping with his manuscript. When I still hadn't heard from him two weeks after our visit, I sent an email to renew my offer. In it, I also asked for a photograph I could include in Sarah's book, and I attached a humorous message that was being passed around the Internet. It was called "Sayings of the Jewish Buddha" and contained epigrams like this:

> Accept misfortune as a blessing. Do not wish for perfect health, or a life without problems. What would you talk about?
>
> The journey of a thousand miles begins with a single *Oy.*

The email was sent at 6PM on January 12, 2009, just two days after I celebrated my birthday. Later that evening, I emailed a copy to Elissa so she would know I was in touch with him and also enjoy the joke. She sent an email back: "I just learned that Rabbi Lew died suddenly today. The funeral will be Thursday. This is too horrible, impossible to comprehend." When I called her, she told me that Rabbi Lew had flown to Baltimore for a conference and was out taking an exercise walk to keep his heart in shape, when it collapsed. He was sixty-five years old.

Perhaps Rabbi Lew would have comprehended this. He was a wise man and he understood that we are born and we die, and that this is the emptiness we seek to fill, and cannot.

Two months later, the family gathered again on the grassy hillside in the cemetery south of San Francisco. We were there for the unveiling of the stone that would mark the spot where we had buried Sarah. Rabbi Lew's fresh grave was nearby, as she would have wanted it.

In the year that had passed the members of our family had drawn closer together as we each reached out for one another in the shadow of her absence. Her spirit was presiding. Rabbi Hyman was there with words to comfort us. Emily had come down again from Washington to sing the *El Molei Rachamin* and a psalm of David. She had made a recording with the psalm and some of her cantorial music and arranged it as a memorial for Sarah. She called the recording "Sarah Laughed." Just before the unveiling she had sent copies to the Seattle congregation with a note:

My best and oldest friend Sarah Horowitz died unexpectedly in March; we buried her on my birthday. I had always associated my birthday with the festival of Purim; now it would be Sarah's *yahrzeit*. The title of this recording, "Sarah Laughed," is from *Parshat Vayera* in which God tells Sarah she will have a son, even though she is very old. Hearing this, Sarah has the *chutzpah* to laugh. She laughs in the face of heaven, in the face of adversity, in the face of propriety. Her sense of humor is one of the ways Sarah *Imenu* is remembered. She did the physically impossible, and was a terrific baker to boot. The chronicle of her death is called "*Chayei* Sarah"—the life of Sarah—because her legacy so overshadows her loss, and her mourners are so comforted by her life, and by the memory of her laughter.

Emily explained that two of the songs she included were texts from the mourning psalms of David. They gave her the words of her grief: "God, what is man that you should know him? The son of mortality, that you should consider him? Man is futility. His days are like a passing shadow."

Another text from the prophet Micah provided her with words for Sarah's legacy, which "must overshadow my grief." It said: "You have been told what is good and what God demands of you: to do justly, to love compassion, and to walk modestly with your God."

Sarah had done all those things, Emily said, "and in the end that is far more important than sadness. Our legacy is the only thing we can really leave our mourners. We have to work to be sure that it is a comforting one."

On the road to the cemetery, a sudden squall cast a rainbow across the heavens, then cleared as swiftly as it had come. A brisk wind put a chill in the air, making it sharper than the year before, and the sky continued its alternations, now grey overcast now brilliant sunlit blue. The bay spring had returned to its normal cycle.

My daughter's headstone was a rose granite and was set under the tree where we had put her in the earth. It was draped in a purple shawl that Emily provided, which had been woven by women in Nepal to benefit orphan children. Next to the stone, a rose bush had been planted at

Elissa's request. On the stone's face was the inscription I had written:

> *She was given*
> *Mountains to climb*
> *Which she did*
> *Lifting all the hearts she touched*